PRAISE FOR KMD89
VA CLAIMS CONSULTING®

"Military transition is difficult, especially navigating the VA disability process. Dewayne made this process easy by reviewing my records, giving me advice on the best approach to my VA claim, and ensuring I knew the process to accurately claim medical impacts from my service. He is the best at what he does. Thanks Dewayne."

–JONATHAN K., Lt. Col. (Ret.), U.S. Army
Special Operations Command

"Dewayne is very passionate about helping Veterans and teaching the VA claims process. I've seen him work on his channel even when he was sick and should have been in bed. You won't find a better person to follow and he is someone we should all strive to emulate in our life."

–TERRY T., U.S. Air Force (Vet.), Electrical Power
Line Specialist

"I HIGHLY recommend KMD89 [VA Claims] Consulting® for assistance with filing your VA claim. I was at my wit's end for many years with this process. I ran across a [KMD89] YouTube video in November 2021, and promptly contacted Mr. Kimble for a consultation the following day. Their method was very different than previous companies I had used. I felt good about the consult, and as a result, I began working with the company in [that same month]. Not only were they extremely patient and accessible, but I was thoroughly educated on the entire process, equipped with the tools needed to file my own comprehensive claim. The key word for me was EDUCATION. Mr. Kimble and DJ genuinely have a heart for Veterans, and it's apparent when speaking to them. I filed my claim at the end of December 2021, and in March 2022, I received my decision letter form the VA (100% P&T)!!! I am so blessed and thankful for the assistance that I received. I encourage you to contact KMD89 for assistance with your VA claim"

— **SONYA B.**, U.S. Air Force (Vet.)

"I wanted to give Mr. Kimble and KMD89 VA Claims Consulting® kudos!!! I have been following his YouTube videos and events. He is very knowledgeable about the VA [claims process]. He takes his time with each question that is asked of him during his events, and he has examples to most questions we veterans ask about our disabilities."

—**ANNETTE B.**, Veteran

"What Dewayne has done and continues to do with all service members and veterans on their VA claims process is inspirational and heartwarming. Dewayne is a subject matter expert in this field, and he does it with so much humility. His 'leave no Vet behind' mantra is something we service members understand, and KMD89 truly embodies this spirit in their support to service members and veterans.

As a veteran myself, I always said that I was very good at being a logistician, but when it comes to VA Claims, I leave it to the professional. All my friends that I recommended to KMD89 have always said one thing: Dewayne is amazing, and they are extremely satisfied with KMD89. If you are still thinking about it, don't. Make the call—it will change your life for the better."

—JUAN S., Commander, JSSD-K

"Dewayne is great!!! He really added value to my VA claims experience. I currently have a pending claim outstanding with the VA and all his advice and coaching made me feel more comfortable with the process, and I have gained both the tools and education to handle my claim going forward. However, Dewayne reminded me that he is always a phone call away. Dewayne's philosophy is: once a client, always a client."

—RAYMOND B., Lt. Cdr., U.S. Navy

" . . . the detail and knowledge of the KMD89 staff has greatly helped me in understanding the claim process. Mr. Dewayne Kimble and his staff go above expectations to assist veterans and their support team with insight of the VA rating process, not only from a VSR or RVSR standpoint but further up to the appeal process."

—**ASHER L.**, U.S. Navy (Vet.)

"Dewayne, today's session on nexus statements was extremely informative and thorough. I left the class with a much better understanding of the importance and details of nexus statements. In addition, I greatly appreciate you spending an additional hour with the attendees to answer any and all questions we had. I highly recommend any and all veterans to take your sessions. I have enrolled in your DBQ session on May 6 (2021). Thank you so much Dewayne."

—**EARL C.**, Veteran

"I reached out to Mr. D. Kimble in order for his company to do an audit on my most recent decision on my claim. The response was very prompt, and he even went out of his way to give me a call to explain the very detailed intricacies regarding my issues. Thank you again Mr. Kimble."

—**MALACHI S. III**, Special Agent, Homeland Security and Sgt., U.S. Army (Vet.)

"I had questions on TDIU, P&T, and SMC and Dewayne Kimble showed me where to find the information that I needed. He also showed me how to get updates from the VA when changes occur. Sir, thank you."

—**STEVEN S.**, Veteran

"Dewayne explained the process from both sides, since he is a veteran and worked for the VA. He encouraged me to ask questions so he could devise the best plan for me. I went from a 0 to 60 percent rating. We are continuing to pursue the 100% rating. He makes this process easier for you. I highly recommend KMD89 for your VA claims.""

— **PERCY V.**, Air Force Crew Chief

VA CLAIMS SUCCESS

YOUR GUIDE TO MAXIMIZING
YOUR VA COMPENSATION BENEFITS

DEWAYNE KIMBLE

To request permission, contact Dewayne Kimble by email at info@kmd89.com.

ISBN Softcover: 978-1-959508-08-3
ISBN Ebook: 978-1-959508-09-0

Book designed by Heidi Caperton

To my grandparents

Mr. and Mrs. AD and Hattie Mae Kimble,

who gave me the best education I could ever have.

TABLE OF CONTENTS

Acknowledgments. . . . . *xvii*

Preface: The Importance of Education. . . . . *xix*

Introduction . . . . *xxvii*

Acronyms . . . . *xxxi*

CHAPTER 1: THE BASICS 1
   Important Regulations & Links 3
   Criteria: The Five Ways of Service Connection 7
   Diagnostic Codes and Rating Percentages 15
   Chapter 1 Checklist 18

CHAPTER 2: BEFORE SEPARATION 21
   Important Regulations & Links 22
   BDD Program Criteria. 24
   Step 1: Get Your Conditions Documented. 27
   Step 2: Get a Copy of Your Medical Records 28
   Step 3: Be 180 to 90 Days from Discharge. 30
   My Big Mistake 31
   Chapter 2 Checklist 33

CHAPTER 3: AFTER SEPARATION 35
   Important Regulations & Links 36
   Criteria. 37

Step 1: Intent to File 38

Step 2: Review Your STRs 44

Step 3: Understand the Rating Criteria 49

Step 4: Gather Additional Evidence 50

Chapter 3 Checklist 57

CHAPTER 4: IMPORTANT FORMS **59**

List of Important Forms 60

VA Claim Form 21-526EZ 63

KMD89's Top 5 Most Common
     Service-Connected Claims 71

Chapter 4 Checklist 80

CHAPTER 5: SUBMITTING YOUR CLAIM **81**

Submit Your Claim. 82

Report to BDD Claim Examinations 86

Report to C&P Examinations (As A Veteran). . . . 87

Freedom of Information Act 97

My Experience with Evidence and Examinations . . . 98

Chapter 5 Checklist 100

CHAPTER 6: YOUR RATING DECISION & NEXT STEPS **103**

Important Forms & Letters 105

How the VA Determines Your Overall
     Disability Percentage 107

Step 1: Wait .109

Step 2: Request a Copy of Your VA Claims Folder . .111

Step 3: Understand Your Notification
     Letter and Rating Decision Letter 113

Step 4: Request Your Disability Breakdown Letter . .117

Next Steps 120

Increase Claim .120
Supplemental Claim 121
Higher-Level Review 122
Board of Veterans' Appeal 125
My Experience with Mistakes and Appeals 127
Final Thoughts .129
Chapter 6 Checklist 130

CHAPTER 7: TIPS & FAQS 133
KMD89's Tips for Success 133
KMD89's Frequently Asked Questions (FAQs) 136

Appendix: Important Resources. 143

Stay Connected with KMD89 VA Claims Consulting® . . . 145

Speaker for Your Next Event 147

LIST OF FIGURES

Figure 1: The Five Ways of Service Connection
Example. 13

Figure 2: Nexus Letter Example 56

Figure 3: VA Form 21-526EZ – Section V:
Claim Information 67

Figure 4: Range of Motion Diagrams for Diagnostic
Code 5237: Lumbosacral or Cervical Strain. 92

Figure 5: Back (Thoracolumbar Spine) Conditions Disability
Benefits Questionnaire (DBQ) 93

Figure 6: Notification Letter Example
(first page only) 114

Figure 7: Rating Decision Letter Example
(first page only) 116

Figure 8: Disability Breakdown Letter Example 119

ACKNOWLEDGMENTS

To Jennifer, my loving wife, who has been an unwavering source of support and inspiration throughout the years. Your belief in me has made all the difference, and I am forever grateful for your encouragement, support, and patience.

To my grandparents and my mother, who instilled in me the drive to pursue my dreams and to never stop learning. You have always been my role models. Your encouragement and guidance have been invaluable in shaping who I am today and the man I have become.

To my uncles, who have been a constant source of guidance, inspiration, and love. I am grateful for the many lessons you taught me and the memories we shared. Thank you for always being there for me and for setting such a wonderful example of what it means to be a caring and responsible man.

To my dear friends, who listened to my ideas, offered constructive feedback, and cheered for me every step of the way. Your support and friendship mean the world to me.

I would like to express my deepest gratitude to all the veterans who served and those currently serving our country. Your selflessness and dedication to protecting our freedom and way of life have not gone unnoticed. All of us at KMD89 VA Claims Consulting® recognize the hardships you endured—the time away from your families, the injuries you sustained, and the memories that will never fade. We are all indebted to you for your service and the sacrifices you made.

And finally, to my readers, who make everything possible. Thank you for your trust, time, and curiosity.

THE IMPORTANCE OF EDUCATION

My grandfather always told me, "Whatever you do, make sure you get your education. You can lose things—your house, your car—but once you have that knowledge, nobody can ever take it away from you." My grandparents raised me in the small, rural town of Charleston in Southeast Missouri. They were fairly poor and didn't get an education beyond grade school. In fact, my grandfather quit school after the third grade, and my grandmother quit in the sixth grade—they had to work in the cotton fields to help support their families. Because they weren't able to finish school, they instilled in me a desire for higher education. I was determined to attend college. Unfortunately, when I called my mom one day (who lived in Chicago, IL) and I told her my goal, she revealed that I didn't have a college fund.

I had no idea what I was going to do.

My grandparents lived near a Missouri National Guard armory—something I'd only vaguely paid attention to as I was growing up. When I realized I didn't have a college fund, the armory suddenly stood out in a whole new light. *This could be my answer.* I scurried in and talked with the recruiter. He told me that, yes, the Guard would help pay for my college. That's all I needed to hear.

I joined the Missouri National Guard as a junior in high school in January 1987. That summer, I attended basic training at Fort Leonard Wood, Missouri. Then, following my high school graduation, I returned to Ft. Leonard Wood for my advanced initial training (AIT) as a 12B Combat Engineer. During that time, I also applied to college.

When my college informational packets started to arrive in the mail, my drill instructor yelled, "You've gotta be kidding me!" Yet one day during mail call, he shouted, "Hey, wait a minute. Kimble, you got a letter from Southeast Missouri State University!" He made me open it right there in front of everyone. My hands shaking, I anxiously unfolded the letter, and found I'd been accepted.

At AIT graduation, the drill instructor pulled me aside and said, "For you to go through all this and apply to college at the same time, that's a great thing. Don't let anything stop you."

And I didn't.

But it wasn't a smooth ride.

During my first year of college in 1989, I pledged Phi Beta Sigma Fraternity, Inc.—and it changed my life. I hadn't taken high school very seriously, so I really struggled in college. My fraternity brothers noticed my grades. "You need to apply yourself," they told me. "You're paying money to get a higher education, and you're representing the fraternity—not just here on this campus, but the entire organization." The upperclassmen were father figures to me. If it wasn't for them, I wouldn't have made college worth my time.

However, keeping up academically was only part of my problems—I was running out of money. One day I drove to the mall to clear my head and noticed an Army recruiting station. I stopped in and connected with a recruiter. By the end of our conversation, I'd decided to go on active duty. In October 1991, I enlisted in the United States Army. I didn't want to leave college or my fraternity brothers, but I had already taken a semester off to work and save money, and I still didn't have enough. So, I went to AIT again, this time to Fort Sill, Oklahoma and was reclassified as a 13C Tactical Automated Fire Control Systems Specialist.

The regular Army sent me to Schweinfurt, Germany. In the National Guard, I had earned the rank of Specialist (E-4); but on active duty, I was a Private (E-2) again. I arrived in Germany in the dead of winter. There I was, doing training exercises out in the field, sleeping in a tent with no heat for several weeks, and truly wondering what the heck I'd signed up for.

Thankfully, a Staff Sergeant (E-6) took an interest in me. I was made Sergeant (E-5) after only two and a half years on active duty. If it weren't for that Staff Sergeant, I never would have gotten promoted that quickly. He taught me how to be a United States Army Soldier, and I am indebted to him for life.

I took college courses on the side during this time. When the Staff Sergeant found out, he started taking classes with me. He once told me, "I've spent fifteen years in the military, and I never took a college course—I've wasted my time!" One of my college instructors actually dropped off tests at the unit's mail room so I could take them with me on field maneuvers. I remember sitting in a Humvee, in the middle of winter again, using a flashlight with a red lens to take a final exam.

My next duty station was Fort Hood, Texas. While there, I was made Staff Sergeant (E-6). And I continued attending college. I encouraged my soldiers to take college courses as well.

I reenlisted for two more years because, at the end of that time, I would be able to attend college full-time for six months after I separated from the Army. So, I originally started college at Southeast Missouri State University in 1988, and I graduated from that same college in 1999. My grandfather had passed away by then, but my grandmother was there for the ceremony. Seeing me graduate from college fulfilled her dream.

I never gave up.

With the Army behind me, I got a corporate job at a large paper manufacturer in Southeast Missouri. I then moved to Chicago to work at a leading food company, where I eventually became a manager. I will never forget my boss in Chicago. He sent me to leadership and safety courses—he groomed me to be a better leader. I looked up to him like I did my Staff Sergeant mentor in the Army.

I later took a manager position back in Missouri, but in an area of the state that was new to me, so I was a little bored. I enrolled in a graduate program and received my MBA from William Woods University.

During my last position in the private sector at a major orange juice company in Florida, a colleague who had served in the Coast Guard asked me one day, "Are you a veteran, and are you getting your compensation benefits?" I didn't even know what compensation benefits were! I had been injured in the service, but I'd never thought much of it.

Little did I know I would soon be working at the U.S. Department of Veterans Affairs.

My first day at the VA was June 2009 as a Rating Veterans Service Representative (RVSR). As an advocate for veterans, working at the VA was one of the most rewarding jobs I ever had. At first, I didn't feel confident enough to ask questions about the disability claims process, so I dove into the VA's manuals and federal regulations and really educated myself.

On my second day on the job, one of my co-workers asked if I was a vet and if I was getting compensated. "What can I claim?" I asked. She replied, "Claim everything you were seen for in the service and everything that's hurting right now." So, I went through the claims process and listed everything I could think of. But as the days went on, I discovered half the things I listed didn't actually meet the VA's criteria for service connection.

In fact, I made three big mistakes with my own claim.

The first mistake was before I even left active duty. I didn't list any injuries or conditions on my separation exam. When I filed a claim as a veteran years later, it was much harder to prove my conditions were service related.

My second mistake was going years without knowing I could receive treatment or compensation from the VA. I didn't educate myself.

Then I made that third mistake—I listed everything without doing any research, which caused me (and the VA) a lot of headaches.

I first filed my claim in June 2009. A year later, I was approved for some things but denied for others. By that time, I had been a VA rater for a while, so I knew I met the criteria for some of the conditions that had been denied. So, I filed another claim... and another ... and another ... but I kept getting denied. That's when I realized not all doctors or VA employees are champions for veterans. It's certainly their job to ensure each claim is valid and to prevent fraud, waste, and abuse; but some go too far and don't really advocate for us.

After years of working on my claim, I felt the VA had turned its back on me, and I decided to file an appeal (now called a higher-level review). During the appeal, which was a conference with a VA Decision Review Officer, the adjudicator kept saying she didn't see the right documentation to prove one of my appealed items. Fortunately, I had kept a copy of everything. I told her exactly where to look. When she saw my included documentation and read it, I won my appeal.

After five long, frustrating years, I finally got approved for everything I had been eligible for.

Though I worked at the VA as a rater, it still took me five years to get what I deserved! I'm lucky I was educated and able to navigate all the red tape. But had I known about the process sooner, I could have avoided a lot of mistakes and saved myself a lot of time and frustration.

Even so, just like with my college degree, I never gave up. I knew if I had made it through the military, college, graduate school, and everything else in my life, I could make it through my VA claims process.

And so can you.

If you do run into issues, I also educate you on how to navigate common obstacles so you can achieve your objective and receive the compensation you deserve.

I've had many clients with horror stories worse than mine, and many veterans feel like giving up. But the one class they never teach in the military is how to quit. And that's what I tell veterans like you every day—don't give up. If you feel you should be 100%, go for it. Whatever you meet the criteria for—10%, 30%, 50%—don't stop until you get it.

I'm going to share with you the federal regulations, VA forms, basic steps, insider tips, and checklists that will help you alleviate problems and disappointments. That doesn't mean it will be smooth or that setbacks won't happen. Everybody's claim is different. But if you take the time to follow this information, I trust you will have a far better experience.

You've served. Now it's time for the VA to serve you.

Don't give up!

ACRONYMS

As we know, the government loves its acronyms. Some of the included acronyms are covered in this book, and some are not. Regardless, they are good to know as you go through the claims process.

- 38 CFR = *Code of Federal Regulations Title 38*
- BDD = Benefits Delivery at Discharge (the process of submitting a claim while still on active duty, 180 to 90 days before discharge)
- BVA = Board of Veterans' Appeals
- C&P Exam = compensation and pension examination, a.k.a. "VA claim exam"
- CAB = Combat Action Badge (Army)
- CAM = Combat Action Medal (Air Force, Space Force)
- CAR = Combat Action Ribbon (Navy, Marines, Coast Guard)
- C-file = claim file
- CIB = Combat Infantryman Badge (Army)

- CMB = Combat Medical Badge (Army)
- COD = character of discharge
- DBQ = Disability Benefits Questionnaire (form used for C&P exams)
- DRO = Decision Review Officer (officer who adjudicates a higher-level review)
- FDC = fully developed claim
- FOIA request = Freedom of Information Act request
- HLR = higher-level review (previously known as an "appeal")
- IDES = Integrated Disability Evaluation System
- M21-1 = *M21-1 Adjudication Procedures Manual*, the reference manual VA employees use to process compensation claims
- MEPS = Military Entrance Processing Station
- MOS = military occupational specialty
- MST = military sexual trauma
- MTF = military treatment facility
- NCA = National Cemetery Administration (part of the VA)
- PA request = Privacy Act request
- PACT Act = Promise to Address Comprehensive Toxics Act
- PMR = private medical records

- PTSD = post-traumatic stress disorder
- RD = rating decision
- RFD = ready for decision
- RMC = Records Management Center
- RO = regional office
- RVSR = Rating Veterans Service Representative
- SCP = special category person (veteran who has suffered loss of a body part)
- SI = seriously injured/ill
- STR = service treatment records (VA term for active-duty medical records)
- VA = U.S. Department of Veterans Affairs (the VA comprises several administrations for various veteran services; the term "VA" is often used interchangeably to mean any VA administration though they serve different functions)
- VAMC = Veterans Affairs Medical Center
- VBA = Veterans Benefits Administration (part of the VA); The VBA not only covers disability compensation benefits but also benefits and services concerning education and training; home loans; life insurance; outreach, transition and economic development; pension; and readiness and employment.

- VHA = Veterans Health Administration (part of the VA, a.k.a. "VA healthcare")
- VSI = very seriously injured/ill
- VSO = veteran service organization/officer
- VSR = Veterans Service Representative

THE BASICS

Whether you're filing your first claim or your fifth claim; whether you're planning to separate or retire from the military or you've been out for thirty years, this book is designed to educate you on the U.S. Department of Veterans Affairs (VA) disability compensation benefits process. I want you to successfully receive the maximum benefits you're eligible for!

If you suffered an injury or illness while serving on active duty, or if a medical (physical or mental) condition has developed or worsened because of your active-duty service, you most likely qualify for monthly, tax-free VA disability compensation benefits. These are benefits that could greatly improve your (and your family's) quality of life.

But you must do the work to prove you have one or more conditions. And you must prove those conditions are connected to your service (the *VA's specific criteria for service connection*, not yours). If you're trying to get "free money" the easiest way possible, this book is not for you. However, if you're willing to put in the work, this book will teach you how to be successful. That being said, everyone's claim is different, every VA rater is different, and every medical examiner is different. That's why education is key.

Each chapter contains some of the most important regulations and/or forms for each type of claim, the basic eligibility criteria, the main steps to follow, and some lessons learned from my own journey as a veteran—a veteran who successfully maximized all of my eligible benefits, and as a retired VA Rating Veterans Service Representative (RVSR).

This will be a lot to take in. Read it in stages. Allow yourself time to absorb the information and do the research you need to do. You may not be able to complete and submit your claim in one day or one week, or even in one month. Your claim is unique to you. Treat this as if you were applying for an in-service school or promotion board. The more work you put into your claim, the easier it will be for the raters to move it onto the next stage.

It's your health and your benefits—compensation benefits that, if approved, you'll receive every month tax-free for the rest of your life. Do the hard work now so you and your family can reap the rewards later.

You made sacrifices to serve your country. You may have been to war and back. You've come this far. Don't give up now.

CHAPTER 1 OVERVIEW

- Important Regulations & Links
- Criteria: The Five Ways of Service Connection
- Diagnostic Codes and Rating Percentages

IMPORTANT REGULATIONS & LINKS

The easiest way to learn how to file a claim is by visiting the U.S. Department of Veterans Affairs website: www.va.gov. Doing an online search of a particular subject within this website (or by using a search engine and clicking on the va.gov results) will help answer many of your questions. You can also visit my YouTube channel (https://www.youtube.com/c/DewayneKimble?sub_confirmation=1, or the QR code) where I cover a lot of details, answer questions, and educate veterans like you about the VA claims process.

The main regulation governing the U.S. Department of Veterans Affairs disability compensation program is the *Code of Federal Regulations Title 38*, commonly referred to as "38 CFR." The chapter regarding disability claims is "Chapter 1, Part 4: Schedule for Rating Disabilities," which you can find in an online search or by using the link provided below.

When you view the main page for Part 4, click on the "table of contents" link. The table of contents menu will provide links to claimable medical conditions separated by body system—such as auditory, endocrine, mental, dental, etc. Also included are the criteria and rating percentages for each. This resource is vital for understanding the criteria for all the conditions you want to claim and at what rating percentages.

To know even more details about how each condition is rated according to the VA's rules, there is also the *M21-1 Adjudication Procedures Manual.* This is the actual reference manual that VA employees use to process compensation claims. It's one of the resources I used as a VA rater, and I still use it today as a consultant to educate my clients.

- VA website for compensation claims, especially: www.va.gov/disability/eligibility/

- 38CFR (especially Chapter 1 Part 4): www.ecfr. gov/current/title-38 - click chapter 1 and scroll down to Part 4

- M21-1: www.knowva.ebenefits.va.gov — hover your cursor over the "Compensation and Pension" menu on the left, then hover over the "M21-1 Adjudication Procedures…" menu, then click on the M21-1 section you want to read , if viewing on your phone, you will have to scroll down.

You'll see these same three resources listed often throughout this book. Don't get overwhelmed—when I went through training as a VA rating specialist, they told us we shouldn't try to memorize all this information. Instead, we should learn its location and how to interpret it as it pertains to the claim we're working on. So, take thirty minutes a day to read this book and reference the regulations as you go through your own claims process. It will save you a lot of time and frustration later.

VA updates to these regulations can and do happen at any time, and those changes may work for you or against you, so it's important to keep reviewing them as you file your claim.

I encourage you to sign up for updates (for both the 38 CFR and M21-1) so you are aware of any changes that could affect your claim before you submit it. You can sign up for email updates by going to the same website as the M21-1. Choose the "Compensation and Pension" tab on the menu on the left. Click on "Subscribe Here" and add your email.

CRITERIA: THE FIVE WAYS OF SERVICE CONNECTION

Anything you claim must be related to your service. So, if you have a condition that doesn't meet one of these five ways of service connection, it *cannot* be considered service connected, and it will not be eligible for compensation.

If I could do my claim over again, I definitely would have researched the five ways of service connection ahead of time. When I worked at the VA as a rating specialist, I adjudicated hundreds of claims. Many claims (like mine at first) listed dozens of conditions, as though the veteran was listing everything they could think of without evidence, hoping something would stick. Sometimes it worked—but only if I, as the rater, could find those conditions listed in their service treatment records (STRs) from active duty. I'll often ask veterans, "For all the things you want to claim, where do they fall under the five ways of service connection?" Often the answer is, "What do you mean?" It's no wonder so many veterans have trouble with their claims. Understanding the five ways of service connection is key.

If you research the five ways of service connection criteria and none of them apply to your claim, you just saved yourself a lot of time and hassle of filing a claim that wasn't eligible in the first place.

If one or more conditions you have does meet the criteria, this information will help you maximize your benefits—you'll be able to understand what the VA is looking for and how to word your claim so it's more likely to be approved.

The five ways of service connection, explained in detail below, are:

1. Pre-Service Aggravation
2. Direct Service Connection
3. Secondary Service Connection
4. Increase Service Connection
5. Presumptive Service Connection

1. Pre-Service Aggravation

This is for a condition you had prior to joining the military that was aggravated or worsened by your active-duty service, as covered in 38 CFR 3.306. For example, I had moderate flat feet (*pes planus*) before I joined the military, which the MEPS examiner noted in my entrance exam. During service, I complained about and was treated for bilateral foot pain. After the military, my doctor noted that I now had *severe* flat feet, which was "at least as likely as not" aggravated by my service. Therefore, my flat feet condition falls under pre-service aggravation.

This phrase "at least as likely as not" is the VA's terminology for proving equal to or greater than a 50% chance that a condition you have is service-connected.

2. Direct Service Connection

In my opinion, this is the most common way veterans claim a service-connected disability. It means you were injured, complained, treated, and/or diagnosed with a particular condition while on active duty, as per 38 CFR 3.304 and 3.305.

A common example is tinnitus, which is ringing in the ears and is often caused by acoustic trauma. So, if your MOS (military occupational specialty) meant that you were around loud noises for long periods of time—such as being on a flight deck, working heavy machinery, or being around artillery—and you did not have a diagnosis of tinnitus before you joined, then your tinnitus could be considered "at least as likely as not" directly caused by your service. I have a video "VA Claim for Tinnitus" on my YouTube channel.

3. Secondary Service Connection

This means you're already service-connected for one condition, and that service-connected condition has caused another, secondary condition. For example, after service, I started having lower back pain. A medical examiner concluded that my flat feet—already service-connected as a pre-service aggravation—were likely causing that lower back pain. Therefore, I submitted a Secondary Service Connection claim for lower back pain, as per 38 CFR 3.310.

4. Increase Service Connection

This is for an increase to your disability compensation percentage for a service-connected disability you've already been granted, either because the condition has worsened, or because you feel you meet the criteria for a higher percentage than you were granted, as per M21-1-II.iii.2.C.1.a. and II.iii.2.C.1.b.

For example, you may have claimed PTSD soon after you got out of the military and were granted 30%. Now, however, the PTSD has worsened and caused more disruption to your daily work and/or personal life, so you file an Increase Claim for a higher percentage.

When doing so, ensure you know the criteria for the next higher percentage (a common mistake veterans make). You can visit my YouTube channel for my video "How to WIN your VA Disability Claim for Increase."

5. Presumptive Service Connection

Presumptive means that if you have one or more conditions and meet the criteria, it is presumed that the condition is service related. This is especially true for certain illnesses like diabetes and cancer since their direct cause is hard to determine. Therefore, if you develop a condition listed in the criteria, and you meet the criteria for having been exposed to one or more toxic substances listed in the criteria while on active duty, it will be presumed that your active-duty service exposed you to a toxic substance—and that exposure caused your condition.

Currently, there are six categories of presumptive conditions (including the PACT Act):

1. 1 Year
2. 3 Year
3. 7 Year
4. Agent Orange
5. Camp Lejeune
6. Gulf War

Because each condition has specific criteria you must meet, it's important to look up the regulations regarding presumptive claims to see if you're eligible, generally 38 CFR 3.307, 3.308, 3.309, 3.318, 3.371, and 3.816. For example, if you think you might have been exposed to Agent Orange while you served on active duty in Thailand, which is a country listed in the Agent Orange criteria, and you're suffering from one or more of the illnesses listed, you may not have enough evidence to prove service connection. If you look closely at the regulation, you will see further details. To meet the Agent Orange exposure criteria, you had to have been in the listed country during certain time frames, spent time in specific locations within that country, and/or performed particular jobs. That's why doing your homework pays off.

The PACT Act, which Congress passed in 2022, greatly expands toxic exposure criteria and illnesses to include Agent Orange, burn pits, respiratory illnesses, cancers, and more. For more information about presumptive conditions, toxic exposure, and the PACT Act, visit the va.gov website and search for "PACT Act."

The chart below is an example illustrating the five ways of service connection.

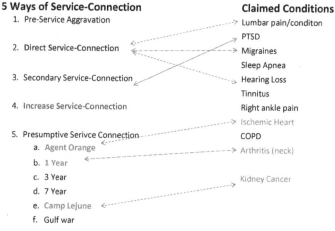

5 Ways of Service-Connection   **Claimed Conditions**

1. Pre-Service Aggravation   Lumbar pain/conditon

                                                     PTSD

2. Direct Service-Connection   Migraines

                                                     Sleep Apnea

3. Secondary Service-Connection   Hearing Loss

                                                     Tinnitus

4. Increase Service-Connection   Right ankle pain

                                                     Ischemic Heart

5. Presumptive Serivce Connection   COPD

   a. Agent Orange   Arthritis (neck)

   b. 1 Year

   c. 3 Year   Kidney Cancer

   d. 7 Year

   e. Camp Lejune

   f. Gulf war

FIGURE I: THE FIVE WAYS OF SERVICE CONNECTION EXAMPLE

In this example, a veteran was treated for a lumbar (lower back) pain condition, migraines, and tinnitus while on active duty. The complaints, diagnoses, and/or treatments for those conditions are listed in the veteran's STRs (service treatment records from active duty). After service, the veteran continues to have issues with those three conditions; therefore, those conditions qualify as Direct Service Connection.

In this same example, the veteran has already claimed and been granted service connection for PTSD, but this condition has worsened and/or caused more difficulty with the veteran's work and/or personal life (or the veteran felt they were not granted the appropriate percentage of compensation and submitted new evidence to be considered for a higher percentage). This is a claim for Increase Service Connection.

The ischemic heart condition (coronary artery disease) is one of the conditions listed under Agent Orange exposure, and this veteran served in a location during a time frame that meets the Agent Orange criteria, so it qualifies as a Presumptive Service Connection.

This veteran also has arthritis in the neck, and the veteran has proof of a diagnosis of arthritis within one year of their discharge date, so it qualifies under the 1-year Presumptive Service Connection criteria.

Finally, the veteran has kidney cancer and was located at Camp Lejeune during the time frame that meets the criteria for having been exposed to contaminated water, so this is also a Presumptive Service Connection.

Hopefully, you can see why doing your research pays off. You may have a condition that meets service-connection criteria, but if you don't do your research, you either a) won't know you qualify for compensation benefits, or b) won't know *how* you qualify and risk getting denied because you didn't know how to properly word your claim.

DIAGNOSTIC CODES AND RATING PERCENTAGES

Once you know which of the five ways of service connection your condition(s) falls under, you should understand the diagnostic codes and rating criteria. This tells you the percentages of compensation for each condition. You'll then know what percentage you are eligible for, how to word your claim, and how to talk to your examiner during your compensation and pension exam (or separation exam, if you're still on active duty).

Keep in mind that you're applying for compensation benefits based on a medical condition you have, so ensuring you understand the VA's terminology is important. A lot of veterans I've worked with over the years just want to tell their story. While I understand that, the VA raters and medical examiners are looking for specific criteria. So if you don't understand the rating criteria, you could cause confusion that might complicate your claim. When writing about your conditions on the VA forms, and when verbally talking about your symptoms during a medical exam if one is warranted, be as clear and concise as possible.

Below are two examples of a condition's diagnostic code and corresponding percentage rating criteria that you'll see when you reference the 38 CFR:

- 8100 Migraine (as per 38 CFR 4.124a)
    - ○ With very frequent completely prostrating and prolonged attacks productive of severe economic inadaptability 50
    - ○ With characteristic prostrating attacks occurring on an average once a month over the last several months 30
    - ○ With characteristic prostrating attacks averaging one in 2 months over last several months 10
    - ○ With less frequent attacks 0

- 7913 Diabetes mellitus (as per 38 CFR 4.119)
    - ○ Requiring more than one daily injection of insulin, restricted diet, and regulation of activities (avoidance of strenuous occupational and recreational activities) with episodes of ketoacidosis or hypoglycemic reactions requiring at least three hospitalizations per year or weekly visits to a diabetic care provider, plus either progressive loss of weight and strength or complications that would be compensable if separately evaluated 100

- ○ Requiring one or more daily injection of insulin, restricted diet, and regulation of activities with episodes of ketoacidosis or hypoglycemic reactions requiring one or two hospitalizations per year or twice a month visits to a diabetic care provider, plus complications that would not be compensable if separately evaluated . . . 60
- ○ Requiring one or more daily injections of insulin, restricted diet, and regulation of activities 40
- ○ Requiring one or more daily injections of insulin and restricted diet, or oral hypoglycemic agent and restricted diet 20
- ○ Manageable by restricted diet only 10

As you can see, the severity of your condition and/or how much it affects your daily life, employment, and more determine what rating percentage you're eligible for.

Make sure you note the words "**and**," which means all criteria are required; and "**or**," which means any one of the criteria listed can count as a requirement. Those little words mean a lot because they change how many requirements need to be met.

You'll also see some rating percentages at 0%, which means you don't get any compensation benefits. *If you think you fall in a 0% rating percentage, still document the condition as service-connected.* If the condition worsens in the future, it's much easier to do an Increase Claim instead of starting a new claim from scratch. So if you have a condition that *only* meets 0% criteria, don't view that as a negative. Make sure to claim it and establish service connection. The 0% criteria are there for a reason.

CHAPTER 1 CHECKLIST

1. Become familiar with the VA website, 38 CFR regulation, and M21-1 reference manual.
2. Determine what conditions you're eligible to claim by understanding the five ways of service connection.
3. Determine what percentage of disability compensation you're eligible to receive for each condition you're claiming by researching the relevant diagnostic codes and rating percentages.

The basic resources, criteria, and information covered in this chapter will be useful as you go through the next steps. This entire book is meant to be a resource, so you'll likely go back and forth through this material as you go through your claims process.

Chapter 2 will cover how to begin a claim if you're still on active duty and planning to separate or retire from the military. If you've already separated, you can learn how to begin your claim by skipping to Chapter 3.

If you've already submitted a claim and have received a rating decision that you do not agree with, or you need to submit another claim (secondary, increase, presumptive, etc.), Chapter 6 will be useful to you, though Chapters 3 through 5 will give you valuable information as well—the more educated you are, the more successful you're likely to be.

BEFORE
SEPARATION

If you're still on active duty, or in the Reserves or National Guard called up to active duty, you can file your disability claim before you leave active-duty service (180 to 90 days before discharge). This process is called the "Benefits Delivery at Discharge" (or BDD program). It enables you to possibly get your disability compensation benefits sooner than if you file after your discharge. More importantly, it allows you to get your conditions documented while you're still on active duty, which greatly helps prove service connection.

If you're closer to your separation date than 90 days, you are excluded from the BDD claims process—but you should go to medical NOW and get all your medical and/or mental injuries, illnesses, pain, and complaints documented, and raise those concerns again during your separation or retirement exam. This is important to prove your injury or illness is related to your time in service. The rest of this book will educate you on how to file a successful claim as a veteran.

CHAPTER 2 OVERVIEW

- Important Regulations & Links
- BDD Program Criteria
- Step 1: Get Your Conditions Documented
- Step 2: Get a Copy of Your Medical Records
- Step 3: Be 180 to 90 Days from Discharge
- My Big Mistake

IMPORTANT REGULATIONS & LINKS

The latest guidance from the Department of Veterans Affairs (VA) covering BDD claims can be found using the resources below. Remember, the VA may change these regulations at any time, so be sure to check for updates:

- The VA website (www.va.gov) and search for "BDD claim" or "Pre-discharge claim"
- 38CFR: www.ecfr.gov/current/title-38 - click chapter 1 and scroll down to Part 4 , and then click on Subpart B "Disability Ratings" Find the body system you are looking for

- M21-1, Part X, Subpart i, Chapter 6, Section B – **Benefits Delivery at Discharge (BDD) and Initial Processing**: www.knowva.ebenefits.va.gov – hover your cursor over the "Compensation and Pension" menu on the left, then hover over the "M21-1 Adjudication Procedures..." menu, then click on the M21-1 section you want to read (listed above) if viewing on your phone, you will have to scroll down

If you can't find the right information based on the regulation number, try searching by chapter title or keywords, as the VA is always changing things.

BDD PROGRAM CRITERIA

To qualify for processing a claim under the BDD program, you must meet *all* the following criteria:

- You're a service member on full-time active duty (including a member of the National Guard, Reserves, or Coast Guard), *and*
- You have a known separation date, *and*
- Your separation date is in the next 180 to 90 days, *and*
- You're available to go to VA exams for 45 days from the date you submitted your claim, *and*
- You can provide a copy of your service treatment records for your current period of service when you file your claim

Don't wait until that 180th day to *start* filing your claim—you want to *submit* your claim on the 180th day. Getting your claim ready with all the supporting documentation takes some time and homework, so plan ahead.

CLAIMS THAT ARE EXCLUDED FROM THE BDD PROGRAM

As per M21-1 X.i.6.B.1.b. and the VA website (at the time of this writing), claims of these types or with any of the attributes listed below are *excluded from the BDD program*, even if service members submit them within 180 to 90 days prior to discharge. You cannot use the BDD program if any *one* of these is true:

- You need case management for a serious injury or illness (such as very seriously injured/ill [VSI], seriously injured/ill [SI], "special category person" [SPC] who suffered loss of a body part, or you are actively enrolled in the Integrated Disability Evaluation System [IDES] program [see M21-1 X.i.6.G.]), *or*
- You are terminally ill, *or*
- You are waiting to be discharged while being treated at a VA hospital or military treatment facility (MTF), *or*
- You are pregnant, *or*

- You are waiting for the government to determine your character of discharge, *or*
- You cannot go to a VA exam during the 45-day period after you submit your claim (subject to the exceptions as per M21-1 X.i.6.B.1.a.), *or*
- You did not submit copies of your service treatment records for your current period of service, *or*
- You have less than 90 days remaining on active duty, *or*
- You added a medical condition to your original claim when you had less than 90 days left on active duty (added conditions will be processed after your discharge), *or*
- You need to have a VA exam done in a foreign country, except if the exam can be requested by the overseas BDD office in either Landstuhl, Germany, or Camp Humphreys, Korea.

Not all discharges are honorable. If a character of discharge (COD) determination needs to be completed by the VA before you can proceed with a claim—don't panic. This doesn't necessarily mean you'll be denied. It depends on the COD determination. Even if your determination denies you from making a BDD claim, you may still be able to file a claim as a veteran. Refer to Chapter

3 to learn more, or review M21-1 X.iv.1.A. – character of discharge (COD) and Bars to Benefits.

Claims requiring a VA examination that must be completed in a foreign country are generally excluded; however, BDD claims will not be excluded when the examination is requested by VA offices in Landstuhl, Germany or U.S. Army Garrison Humphreys (Camp Humphreys), Korea, as those examinations can be completed in multiple foreign countries.

STEP 1:
GET YOUR CONDITIONS DOCUMENTED

For your entire military career, whether it was two years or two decades or more, you were told to "suck it up and drive on." But now that you're planning to leave the military, it's time to start taking care of yourself. If you are suffering from an illness, injury, disease, pain, or other condition or complaint, go to medical and get it documented. If you're coming up on your separation exam, list everything that is an issue or could be a problem in the future. *Don't suck it up!* If a condition is not documented in your STRs (service treatment records from active duty), it will be harder to prove service connection after you've separated from the military.

Do not put this off. This is not the time to be tough.

If it's not documented and you feel it should be, get it documented. If you feel you may have sleep apnea, you *must* get a sleep study while you're on active duty and receive a diagnosis of sleep apnea for it to be service related. (Sleep apnea is covered in detail in Chapter 4.) If you have a parachutist badge and you have back aches, shoulder aches, neck pain, or joint pain (knees, elbows, wrists, ankles), get that documented. Don't wait. *Once you're no longer in the service, it becomes much harder to prove a condition you have is service related.*

STEP 2:
GET A COPY OF YOUR MEDICAL RECORDS

You should request a full copy of your STRs (service treatment records) from the medical facilities where you are stationed on active duty. The VA will not have a copy of your STRs yet since you haven't yet separated, so submitting the relevant documents as evidence with your BDD claim is necessary to prove service connection. While getting a copy of your STRs is a regular part of the discharge process, you can request a copy even before you begin separating or retiring.

Get a copy early so you can go through it and assess all your complaints, diagnoses, injuries, diseases, illnesses, chronic pain, and treatments. If an illness or injury is currently bothering you, or one or more illnesses/injuries wasn't documented, go to medical and get it documented *now*.

If a condition you have is already documented, you still want to bring it up in your separation exam. The easier a condition is to find in your STRs, the easier it will be to prove your claim.

When reviewing your STRs, look specifically for the complaints you had for each appointment, what was diagnosed, and what the treatment plan was. If you have trouble with this, KMD89 VA Claims Consulting® provides educational webinars, Service Treatment Record Reviews, and other educational services you can access at: www.kmd89.com/services.

Noting your complaints, diagnoses, and treatments will make the BDD process that much faster and less frustrating for you and the VA.

If you were treated by a private medical or mental health professional while you were on active duty, you can submit a copy of those documents as evidence to help support your claim. You can also bring the relevant documents with you to your separation exam if you think it will help the medical examiner understand your condition(s).

For more information on STRs, review M21-1 III. ii.2.A.1.e. and III.ii.2.A.1.f.

STEP 3:
BE 180 TO 90 DAYS FROM DISCHARGE

You should know the month and year you're planning to separate or retire from the service. Plan ahead so you can submit your claim and all supporting documentation on your *180th day from discharge*, which leaves you more time for your medical exams. Even if you're still a few years out, now is the time to start ensuring everything is documented.

You'll have a lot of other things going on during your discharge process, like clearing government housing, packing for a move, preparing for terminal leave, and so on—especially if you're overseas or planning to travel.

Go to sick call or medical and get any issues documented. If a supervisor questions you, tell them you're preparing to separate or retire, and you need to ensure your medical records are accurate. It will soon be time for another service member to step up and carry the load.

If you've passed the 180-day mark but are still before the 90th day, go ahead and do what you can. Sooner is always better than later.

If you've passed the 90th day, you are excluded from the BDD claims process—but *now* is the time to go to sick call and get everything documented. This will become evidence to prove that your injury or illness was documented during service. Once you're no longer in the service, it becomes much harder to prove your condition is service related. Now is also the time to educate yourself on the criteria so you can file a successful claim as a veteran, as covered in Chapter 1.

MY BIG MISTAKE

I received a bad piece of advice when I was separating from the military. In fact, no one told me about VA disability compensation benefits at all; there was no briefing about VA benefits back then during the discharge process. When I completed my separation exam, someone told me I shouldn't mark "Yes" for any injuries or issues. They said that if I did, I'd be held for a couple of days for more medical exams. I didn't want to stay any longer than I had to, so I checked "No" for everything. That was a *big* mistake.

I should have been accurate and checked "Yes" for all the conditions and injuries I had from service or that had been aggravated by my service. Looking back on it now, I'd already spent years on active duty, so another twenty-four or forty-eight hours would not have been a big deal. I then would have had proper documentation that proved I had service-connected issues—and that would have *saved me several years* of filing and fighting for my claim later on as a veteran.

After I filed my claim as a veteran and went to my first compensation and pension exam, the examiner said, "You didn't note anything on your separation exam. And when you were on active duty, you were only seen once or twice for this." So initially I got denied for things I knew were service related, and it took me years to get approved for everything I was eligible to receive.

That's why I'm so adamant about going to medical and getting your issues documented before you get out. When you're leaving the service, you're probably ready to move on as quickly as possible. But taking care of your health and getting it documented before discharge will help protect your future.

CHAPTER 2 CHECKLIST

1. Be familiar with the VA's website, 38 CFR, and M21-1.
2. Understand the criteria for submitting a claim under the BDD program.
3. Go to medical and get your conditions documented, and list all your injuries, illnesses, diseases, and complaints during your separation exam.
4. Get a copy of your Service Treatment Records (STRs, or active-duty medical records) no matter how long you've been in, including any treatment from a private facility (while you were on active duty).
5. Be 180 to 90 days from your discharge date.

This chapter covered how to complete and submit your Benefits Delivery at Discharge (BDD) claim. However, you may need to file another claim as a veteran, and every claim is different. There are situations you may encounter and information you may need that's not covered in this chapter. I encourage you to keep reading this book and keep reading the VA regulations and references listed, so you can avoid frustration and maximize your VA compensation benefits.

If you need further education or clarification, contact KMD89 VA Claims Consulting®. It's our mission to educate service members like you.

Don't give up!

AFTER SEPARATION

If you're filing a new claim, or you've already submitted an increase, presumptive, or secondary claim as a veteran after your first claim (or BDD claim), this chapter will get you started.

CHAPTER 3 OVERVIEW

- Important Regulations & Links
- Criteria (for filing a claim as a veteran)
- Step 1: Intent to File
- Step 2: Review Your STRs
- Step 3: Understand the Rating Criteria
- Step 4: Gather Additional Evidence

IMPORTANT REGULATIONS & LINKS

Below are the main regulations you'll need to reference to start filing your claim.

- The VA website (www.va.gov), where you can search for "Intent to File" and "How to File a Claim"

- 38 CFR (www.ecfr.gov/current/title-38), especially "Part 3, Subpart A – How to File a Claim," (click chapter 1 and scroll to 3.155) and "Part 4 – Schedule for Rating Disabilities" (click chapter 1 and scroll down to Part 4)

- M21-1 Manual Reference: www.knowva.ebenefits.va.gov – hover your cursor over the "Compensation and Pension" menu on the left, then hover over the "M21-1 Adjudication Procedures ..." menu, then click on the M21-1 section you want to read (or do a keyword search in the search menu) if viewing on your phone, you will have to scroll down

Keep in mind these regulations are always being updated, so make sure you double-check them prior to submitting your claim. If you can't find the right information based on the regulation number, try searching by chapter title or keywords.

CRITERIA

As stated on the VA's website (at the time of this writing and subject to change), you MAY qualify for VA disability compensation if you meet the below requirements (depending on the VA's decision):

Both of these must be true:

- You have a current illness or injury (known as a condition) that affects your mind or body, *and*
- You served on active duty, active duty for training, or inactive duty training

AND at least *one* of these must be true:

- You got sick or injured while serving in the military—and can link this condition to your illness or injury (called an in-service disability claim), *or*
- You had an illness or injury before you joined the military—and serving made it worse (called a pre-service disability claim), *or*
- You have a disability related to your active-duty service that didn't appear until after you ended your service (called a post-service disability claim)

If you think you meet these requirements, follow the steps below to file your claim.

STEP 1:
INTENT TO FILE

The first step as a veteran filing a VA disability compensation claim is to do an Intent to File (if not on active duty). While voluntary, this step creates your (possible) claim's effective date and gives you a year to submit your formal claim without penalty. This allows you time to gather all the supporting documentation needed so you can submit everything at once (as a fully developed claim, or FDC). In essence, it allows you to be compensated for the research and time it took you to gather the appropriate evidence for your claim, rather than just for the time it took the VA to approve your claim. This means that if your claim is approved, you could be compensated with back pay for the entire period from the Intent to File (effective) date to the VA's approval date, in addition to the monthly benefits you receive from then on.

If you *do not* do an Intent to File, the effective date will be the date the VA received your claim (also known as date of claim), which should be the date you submitted it (though there are exceptions depending on what you're claiming; sometimes an effective date will be "date facts found"). This is why I encourage you to keep a copy of all documentation you send to and receive from the VA. Keep proof of effective dates along with all correspondence, evidence submitted, and everything else related to your claim, which can help you if any issues arise. (The Intent to File replaces the informal claims process; the VA stopped accepting informal claims on March 24, 2015.)

However, if you do an Intent to File but don't submit a claim within that 365-day window, the Intent to File will expire, and you will not receive any back pay from the Intent to File date. (You may still be eligible to receive back pay from the date the VA received your claim if you are granted service connection.)

There are several ways to do an Intent to File. The main ways are listed below:

1. Call the VA benefits hotline (VA national call center) at **1-800-827-1000** and tell them you would like to do an Intent to File for compensation.

    a. You should receive a letter in the mail confirming your Intent to File a few days or weeks after you make this phone call. You may also get an email within 24 hours with information about VA benefits, but this is not the same as the letter. The letter is your confirmation—make a copy of it when you receive it, and keep it with all your other claim documents.

    b. You may want to call the number again a week later to verify they documented your Intent to File date and that your letter is in the mail—this could save you a month or two of back pay.

2. Or start filing your claim on the VA's website but do not submit it.

    a. Go to www.va.gov, search for "How to file a claim," scroll down to the green arrow and click on the link that says, "File a disability compensation claim online," then click on the blue link that says, "Sign in to start your application."

b. Sign in using your ID.me, My HealtheVet, or other credentials.

c. Start filling out the information.

d. Click on "Finish this application later" to save the application—when an electronic application is initiated and saved in a VA web-based electronic claims application system, the VA will consider that saved application to be an Intent to File a claim.

e. Once you have saved your application, you should see a gray box that specifies the date when you must complete your application, which should be 365 days from your Intent to File date. This is a good way to check that your Intent to File date is in the VA's records.

3. Or fill out an Intent to File form using **VA Form 21-0966** "Intent to File a Claim for Compensation and/or Pension, or Survivors Pension and/or DIC," which you can find on the VA's website (www.va.gov) by searching for "VA Form 21-0966."

a. Submit **VA Form 21-0966** using Quick-Submit on the VA's website: https://eauth.va.gov/accessva/#forVeterans. Sign in with your ID.me, My HealtheVet, or other credentials as listed, click on the blue "*Quick-Submit*" tab, double check that your name, SSN, and zip code are correct, and attach/upload your completed **VA Form 21-0966**.

4. Or submit **VA Form 21-0966** via mail to:
    Department of Veterans Affairs
    Evidence Intake Center
    P.O. Box 4444
    Janesville, WI 53547-4444

Note that all you need to do is state you're intending to file for compensation or pension. The VA does not need any other information, and they should not ask you about specific benefits or conditions you're claiming at this stage.

The first option is the easiest for most veterans. No matter how you do your Intent to File, you should receive

a letter confirming your Intent to File. If you do not receive this letter in a few weeks, follow up with the VA by
calling the VA benefits hotline/national call center again
(1-800-827-1000). This could save you several months
of back pay rather than waiting for a letter that never
arrives. If you are granted service connection, the VA pays
by the month, so every month counts. If you do an Intent
to File on November 1st and your claim is approved on
December 2nd, the back pay will be the for the month
of November. But if you do an Intent to File on October
31st and your claim is approved on December 2nd, you'll
get back pay for both October and November.

Once you get your Intent to File letter, keep a copy
of it with all your other claim documents. That way you're
not penalized if the VA gets the effective date wrong, or
they take longer than usual at some point in the process.

The Intent to File can really help if it takes a while to
submit your claim. I know one veteran who got back pay
for eleven months, and since he was approved for 90%
disability compensation benefits, he received a lump sum
payment of around $30,000. Unfortunately, that makes
some veterans think they can do an Intent to File and
then wait a year to submit their claim, but it's the same
amount of money either way. If it takes longer for you to
gather the evidence you need, or you end up waiting too
long, your Intent to File could expire. Furthermore, the

VA is always changing things, so the longer you wait, the more trouble you could run into. You never know what might happen. This is why it's good to sign up for the regulation updates and to keep checking the regulations before you submit your claim, and why it's good to submit your claim as soon as you've done all the research and gathered all the evidence you need.

While you have 365 days to submit your claim, the VA does not have a deadline as to when they approve or deny it. So, the faster you submit, the better off you'll be. You want as much time within that year to go to your exams, submit any further evidence the VA requests, fix any issues, or follow up with any VA delays.

STEP 2:
REVIEW YOUR STRS

You should already have a copy of your STRs (service treatment records from active duty). If you don't, you can request a copy from the VBA (Veterans Benefit Administration) using **VA Form 20-10206** "Freedom of Information Act (FOIA) or Privacy Act (PA) Request." You can download this form after searching for it on the VBA's website (www.va.gov). Once you have read the instructions and filled out the form completely, you can submit it to the VBA in the following ways:

- Online via *Quick*Submit (AccessVA)
    - o Go to VA QuickSubmit (or Direct Upload via AccessVA) or search for "QuickSubmit" on the VA's website (www.va.gov)
    - o Sign in with the appropriate credentials (there are several ways to log in)
    - o Click on the blue "*Quick*Submit" tab
    - o Double-check that your name, SSN, and zip code are correct
    - o Attach/upload your completed and signed **VA Form 20-10206**
    - o For a step-by-step tutorial on *Quick*Submit, watch my YouTube video "VA *Quick*Submit Claim - How to expedite your VA Claim to the VA"

- Or *Mail* your completed VA Form 20-10206 in an envelope to:
  Department of Veterans Affairs
  Evidence Intake Center
  P.O. Box 4444
  Janesville, WI 53547-4444

If the VA doesn't have your STRs or if you have never filed a claim, you can request them from the National Archives online via www.archives.gov/veterans, or by filling out **Standard Form 180 (SF 180)** "Request Pertaining to Military Records" and following the instructions. You can also download a copy of **SF 180** using the National Archives website. (**SF 180** is set to expire April 30, 2024, so these links and instructions may change.)

If you have a milConnect account, you can log in, click on "Correspondence/Documentation," select "Defense Personnel Records Information (DPRIS)" from the drop-down menu, choose the "Personnel File" tab, and select "Request My Personnel File." Fill out the form, and in the "Document Index" section, check the boxes next to the document(s) you'd like to request. Finally, click on the "Create and Send Request" button.

When you have a copy of your STRs, go through them and note all your complaints, diagnoses, injuries, diseases, illnesses, chronic pain, and everything you were treated for on active duty. If you have trouble with this, KMD89 VA Claims Consulting® provides educational webinars, Service Treatment Record

Reviews, and other educational services you can access at: www.kmd89.com/services.

You may think it's up to the VA raters who go through your records, but trust me—as someone who was a rater with the VA, you don't want to leave it up to them. Raters are often backlogged and have deadlines and quotas to meet, and some claims are hundreds and hundreds—even thousands—of pages long, so details are easy to miss. It's their job to make sure each claim is valid, so don't leave them with any questions or doubts.

If you take the time to look through your STRs, you can find the main pages that contain the complaints, diagnoses, and treatments for the condition(s) you're claiming. Submit those documents as evidence to help your claim go through the process as smoothly and quickly as possible. Remember, this is not the time to do the bare minimum and hope the VA sympathizes with you.

The VA has too many other claims to process. This is *your* claim for your compensation benefits, possibly for the rest of your life, so put in the work to help yourself as much as possible.

On the flip side, you don't want to submit too much. If you submit all the files you have without actually assessing them, you're basically doing nothing. As a rater, I often had *thousands* of pages to look through, and it was like searching for a needle in a haystack.

Gathering the relevant documents and highlighting the most important information will help make the claims process that much faster and less frustrating for you and for the VA. Do the hard work now so you can reap the rewards later.

For more information on STRs, review M21-1 III.ii.2.A.1.e. and III.ii.2.A.1.f.

STEP 3:
UNDERSTAND THE RATING CRITERIA

The next step is to understand how each condition you're claiming falls under the five ways of service connection, and what percentage of compensation you are eligible for based on the criteria as per 38 CFR Part 4, Schedule for Rating Disabilities, as covered in Chapter 1.

A service member I consulted with was frustrated that he had been denied for knee pain. But, he never specified whether it was his right or left knee, nor did he follow up with the VA regarding which knee it was. Remember, you're submitting a disability compensation claim based on a medical condition. You need to be specific and word your claim as close as possible to the rating criteria it falls under. Reading the regulations is so important—this knowledge will not only help you word your claim but prevent confusion during your compensation and pension exam. Furthermore, as you research your claim, you'll see what other evidence you may need or want to submit to increase your chances of success.

It's usually best to submit a fully developed claim (FDC), which means you submit the claim form and all other relevant evidence at the same time. An FDC helps the VA raters process your claim efficiently and can expedite the process.

STEP 4:
GATHER ADDITIONAL EVIDENCE

There are certain conditions you can claim without medical evidence, though you need to do your research first. Some examples are joint pain if you have a parachutist badge (generally ankles, knees, hips, and/or back), tinnitus (due to acoustic trauma), military sexual trauma (MST) (discussed later in Chapter 4; if you have evidence of a stressor event or marker), and many presumptive conditions (Agent Orange, Camp Lejeune Contaminated Water, Gulf War Undiagnosed Illness, or toxic exposure under the PACT Act), depending on the criteria. The threshold criteria for certain conditions are lower than for others. For instance, the VA understands that many veterans dealing with PTSD or MST didn't bring up those issues while on active duty. Veterans may still not feel comfortable raising them now, especially if they have trust issues with the VA. So, while some VA raters may argue they don't see anything in your STRs, you can argue your case if you know the regulations.

VA HEALTHCARE PROGRESS NOTES

If you've received healthcare services from a VA medical facility after your active-duty service for the condition(s) you're claiming, the VA also has access to those medical records (electronically back to the mid-2000s), which are called "VA progress notes." While the VA raters are supposed to look at both your STRs and VA progress notes, make sure to review your own VA progress notes. Gather and highlight the relevant documents, complaints, diagnoses, and treatments, just as I mentioned earlier with your STRs.

To access your VA progress notes, along with other VA Healthcare tools, you should register for "My HealtheVet" at www.myhealth.va.gov (if you haven't done so already).

Vet Center records, however, are *not* accessible through the VA. Request a copy of those yourself from the Vet Center where you were seen. Or, go through the Veteran Benefits Administration (VBA) and have them make a request for you via **VA Form 21-4142** "Authorization to Disclose Information to the Department of Veterans Affairs." (Though the process is much faster if you request them yourself.)

PRIVATE MEDICAL RECORDS (PMR)

Though not necessary, if you have medical records from outside of active duty and outside of the VA, especially from a private/civilian provider, this evidence can help. (As mentioned, this includes any progress notes from a Vet Center, as those records are separate from the VA Medical Center.)

Remember to submit only the most relevant information, especially the complaints, diagnoses, and treatments as discussed previously. Though this is your claim, so only you can be the judge of what you want to submit.

OTHER DOCUMENTS

Other military documents, such as badges, awards, certificates, orders, and more can be used to support your claim.

You could provide a combat action badge (CAB) or equivalent (as discussed later in Chapter 4) to support your claim for combat-related PTSD. You could submit a copy of an award or certificate that states the specific base or location you served at in support of a presumptive claim for Agent Orange. Or you could submit a diagnosis that is on the criteria for Agent Orange, Camp Lejeune Contaminated Water, Gulf War Undiagnosed Illness, or toxic exposure under the PACT Act. (Be sure to review the required criteria for each presumptive.)

PUBLIC DBQ EXAMS & NEXUS LETTERS

After you submit your claim, the VA will generally schedule you for a medical examination to verify your condition(s) and determine the residuals. This exam is called a "Compensation and Pension Exam," commonly referred to as a "C&P exam." However, you *can* have a private provider of your choice do a C&P exam instead of a VA-directed provider (in most cases). The required paperwork for all C&P exams is a Disability Benefits Questionnaire (DBQ). Sometimes a medical opinion and rationale supporting service connection, called a Nexus

Statement or Nexus Letter, is also required to prove service connection.

A C&P exam that is not VA-directed but instead is completed by a provider of your choice, at your own cost, is commonly referred to as a "public DBQ," or just "DBQ exam," while a VA-directed exam is commonly referred to as a "C&P Exam." (This is despite the fact all C&P exams use the DBQ paperwork whether they are requested by you or by the VA.)

If you prefer your own provider to complete your C&P exam(s), you'll need to submit the proper DBQ paperwork as evidence *at the same time you submit your claim*, not after. Otherwise, the VA will still schedule you for a C&P exam, and you may have wasted your time and money. If you plan to do this, I provide more information about C&P exams in Chapter 5. (First, you have to ensure your provider of choice understands and is willing to complete a VA C&P exam/public DBQ.)

It's important you are educated on which DBQ you need. Different categories of conditions require different DBQs. You may even require more than one DBQ if you require different specialists for your various conditions. Always go to the VA's website, search for "DBQ," and find the page that lists the DBQs for each medical category, which you can download. That way you can view the correct DBQ form ahead of time for each condition you're claiming (the DBQs are updated from time to time, so you may want to check back before your exam to ensure you have the latest DBQ).

If you're filing an Initial or Secondary claim that is *not a Presumptive* claim, the provider must usually also write a Nexus Letter, which is a statement from the examiner giving their opinion on whether or not your condition(s) is "at least as likely as not" caused or aggravated by your military service and a rationale for their opinion.

The Nexus Statement should include the veteran's name, SSN, date, diagnosis, the documents reviewed, the specialist's medical opinion of your condition(s), the severity of the condition(s), and the rationale for their opinion.

An example of a medical opinion and rationale may be, "The veteran's current symptoms are logically related to and consistent with the medical problems being reported. Based on this examination, the veteran meets diagnostic criteria for a [diagnosis]. The [diagnosis] is at least as likely as not (51 percent or greater probability) incurred in or caused by [claimed in-service injury/event/illness] due to or the result of the veteran's health treatment noted in their military service treatment records. The opinion is based on my review of all records, the clinical interview with the veteran, the diagnostic criteria as described in [medical manual]; along with my clinical training, experience, interview with the veteran, and judgment." A full Nexus Letter example is also provided below.

Company Letterhead

RE: [veteran's name]
DOB: [month/date/year]
Type of Medical Opinion: Secondary

To Whom it May Concern,

I am [list medical or mental professional name] providing the following nexus.

Medical Opinion:

It is my medical opinion, as a [list profession], that the veteran's current diagnosis of [List diagnosis] is least as likely as not, (more than 51 percent probability) due to or the result of the veteran's service-connected [list service-connected condition].

Rational:

The veterans VA claim file/e-folder and private treatment records were reviewed.

Results of a self-report measure and clinical interview are consistent with [list diagnosis].

The veteran's current symptoms are logically related to and consistent with [list diagnosis]. Also, the veteran's current symptoms are logically related to and consistent with the medical problems being reports.

The veteran has multiple reports of [list diagnosis] that have worsened over time. According to the studies conducted by [list any medical studies/medical literature/articles etc.].

A medical [list any medical studies/medical literature/articles etc.].

Also, the condition is permanent and progressive in nature.

Sincerely,

Dr. John Doe
License and/or NPI#

FIGURE 2: NEXUS LETTER EXAMPLE

The VA will verify your healthcare provider's credentials when reviewing your claim. You need to ensure you get all the proper DBQs and Nexus Letters completed by the proper specialists for all the conditions you're claiming. If you don't, the VA will schedule you for any specific C&P exams you need for conditions you're claiming that don't already have an actionable and sufficient public DBQ.

Some veterans who were frustrated with VA-directed C&P exams successfully utilized the public DBQ process with medical professionals of their choice after they became our clients. I wish it wasn't the case, but unfortunately, not all C&P examiners (or VA raters) are obvious advocates for veterans. But many of them are, so the choice is yours.

CHAPTER 3 CHECKLIST

1. Be familiar with the VA's website, 38 CFR, and M21-1.
2. Determine if you meet the criteria for filing a claim as a veteran.
3. Complete an Intent to File so you are not penalized financially for reviewing material and gathering evidence to support your claim.

4. Understand the rating criteria for each condition you're planning to claim.

5. Review your active-duty service treatment records (STRs).

6. Gather any additional evidence and/or request a C&P exam from a private healthcare facility of your choice (if you do not want a VA-directed C&P exam after you file your claim).

7. Don't quit!

IMPORTANT FORMS

You would think filling out the forms would be easy, but you're dealing with the government. Take your time and do your research. Remember, certain conditions you claim may require additional forms. This chapter will cover all the form basics, as well as specific guidelines for claiming the top five most common service-connected claims I've seen, which are sleep apnea, tinnitus, migraines, joint pain, and PTSD (including combat-related PTSD, non-combat PTSD, and personal trauma PTSD).

CHAPTER 4 OVERVIEW

- List of Important Forms
- VA Claim Form 21-526EZ
- KMD89's Top 5 Most Common Service-Connected Claims

LIST OF IMPORTANT FORMS

These are some of the forms you may need when filing your claim:

- **DD214** "Certificate of Release or Discharge from Active Duty"
  - ○ While the VA should have a copy of this (if you've already separated or retired from the military), it's important to review when filing your claim.
  - ○ If you've already retired or separated and can't find a copy of your DD214, you can request it (and other documents) on the VA website (www.va.gov).
- **VA Form 21-526EZ** "Application for Disability Compensation and Related Compensation Benefits"—the most common form when applying for VA disability benefits because it is used for:

- o All initial claims
- o Pre-Service Aggravation
- o Direct Service Connection
- o Secondary Service Connection
- o Increase Service Connection
- o Presumptive Service Connection
- o Certain types of special monthly compensation (SMC)
- o Temporary claims for paragraphs 29 and 30 benefits
- **VA Form 21-4138** "Statement in Support of Claim"
  - o This form is an optional form that can be used to further support your claim, as either a "buddy statement" or "lay statement" where someone else writes a statement on your behalf, or as an addition to **VA Form 21-526EZ** that allows you to better explain your conditions, how they connect to your service, and how they affect your daily life.
- **VA Form 21-0781** "Statement in Support of Claim for Service Connection for Post-Traumatic Stress Disorder (PTSD)," and **VA Form 21-0781a** "Statement in Support of Claim for Service Connection for Post-Traumatic Stress Disorder (PTSD) Secondary to Personal Assault"

- ○ If you're planning to claim PTSD that is *not directly related to combat*, you may need one or both of these forms.
- ○ **VA Form 21-0781** is generally used for combat or non-combat PTSD; **VA Form 21-0781a** is used for personal trauma PTSD (both are discussed later in this chapter).
- **VA Form 21-686c** "Application Request to Add and/or Remove Dependents"
  - ○ Add or remove dependents from your benefits (to add dependents to an existing claim, you have to be service-connected at least 30%).
- **VA Form 21-8940** "Veteran's Application for Increase Compensation Based on Unemployability," and **VA Form 21-4140** "Employment Questionnaire"
  - ○ Individual unemployability is not a standalone claim, but an increase in condition(s) you've already claimed that affect your ability to keep a steady job.
- **VA Form 21-2680** "Examination for Housebound Status or Permanent Need for Regular Aid and Attendance"

- º Special Monthly Compensation for Regular Aid and Attendance (SMC-L) and Housebound (SMC-S), for which the criteria can be found in 38 CFR 3.350(b) (1), (2), & (3) (for service-connected conditions only).
- **VA Form 20-0995** "Decision Review Request: Supplemental Claim"
  - º When you are denied a claim and want to reopen that claim, you will need to submit this form, covered more in Chapter 6 (please read the form's instructions for additional evidence that needs to be submitted).

VA CLAIM FORM 21-526EZ

Now that you know what conditions you're claiming, the criteria and rating percentage you meet for each condition, and you have the evidence needed to back up your claim, it's time to fill out the claim form. The form at the time of this writing is **VA Form 21-526EZ** "Application for Disability Compensation and Related Compensation Benefits" (subject to change with VA regulation updates).

You can download a copy from the VA's website by searching for "VA Form 21-526EZ," then save it to your computer, fill it out, and submit it along with your evidence.

Or you can start filling out the form on the VA's claim website as discussed in Chapter 3 (Go to www.va.gov, search "How to file a claim," scroll down to the green arrow and click on the link that says, "File a disability compensation claim online," then click on the blue link that says, "Sign in to start your application"). With this second method, you don't see the form. Instead, you are prompted to answer a series of questions, and when you're finished, the form automatically populates for you. You *must remember to save your progress before logging out* each time you update the form. Otherwise, you may lose your progress and have to start over, or you may end up submitting an incomplete form.

Personally, I feel this online version is a bit confusing, which is why I recommend downloading the form and filling it out that way. This also allows you to look over the entire form and read the form's instructions before you fill it out.

When you download **VA Form 21-526EZ**, you'll see that it's fifteen pages long. The first eight pages are instructions. A lot of veterans skip the instructions and just start filling out the form, but the instructions are there for a reason. Any mistakes you make, no matter how small, can increase the chances your claim will be denied, causing you more work later. You've done the research to get this far. Don't fill out the form incorrectly or leave anything blank because you didn't follow the instructions.

The form mentions the ability to contact a veteran's service organization or Veterans Service Officer (VSO) for assistance. I've known veterans who have used VSOs. Some VSOs are really good, while others don't take the time to educate the veteran on their claim or do their due diligence to assist the veteran. For example, some veterans who used VSOs contacted KMD89 VA Claims Consulting® afterward—they still had issues or confusion with their claim. That's why I recommend educating yourself and taking ownership of your claim even if you use a VSO. You'll be more aware if the VSO is really helping you or not.

One of the next things you'll see on the form is an option to either submit your claim using the fully developed claim program (FDC) or the Standard Claim Process. FDC means you submit everything necessary for the VA to move forward with your claim, *and* you have nothing else to submit. A Standard Claim means you're not finished and have additional evidence to submit, so the VA should *not* move forward right away (the form gives detailed instructions on the Standard Claim Process).

Because of the Intent to File (as explained in Chapter 3), there's really no reason for you to submit a Standard Claim. The Intent to File allows you 365 days to do your research, fill out the proper form(s), gather any evidence, and submit everything at the same time as a fully developed claim. If your claim is approved and you are granted compensation benefits, the VA will possibly award you a lump sum of back pay up to that Intent-to-File date (though each claim is different).

However, if you submit an FDC claim but do not submit all the evidence needed according to the criteria applicable to your claim, or you submit additional evidence after filing an FDC claim, it will be removed from FDC status and become a Standard Claim.

When I was a rater, I saw some FDC claims that were missing information, and some Standard Claims that were complete. I started on the claims that were complete regardless of what they were called. This is because many veterans don't know what evidence they need to submit, or worse yet, don't know if their conditions meet the criteria for service connection. So, if you're a veteran (no longer on active duty), make sure you read Chapter 3 so you can submit a fully developed claim.

Next on the form's instructions, you'll read about special circumstances, which often require additional forms, such as **VA Form 21-0781** or **VA Form 21-0781a**

for PTSD (more on PTSD later in this chapter under "KMD89's Top 5 Most Common Service-Connected Claims").

After reading all the instructions, you'll start filling out your basic information. It's important to fill out each block as it applies to you—don't skip anything unless it tells you to. It's best to find a quiet spot, take your time, and fill it out slowly so you don't make any mistakes. If you get confused, take the time to review the instructions and regulations again.

When you get to "Section V: Claim Information," you'll see three examples listed (as shown below in "Figure 3").

EXAMPLES OF DISABILITIES	EXAMPLES OF EXPOSURE	EXAMPLES OF HOW THE DISABILITY(IES) RELATES TO SERVICE	EXAMPLES OF DATES
EXAMPLE I: HEARING LOSS	NOISE	HEAVY EQUIPMENT OPERATOR IN SERVICE	JULY 1968
EXAMPLE 2: DIABETES	AGENT ORANGE	SERVICE IN VIETNAM WAR	DECEMBER 1972
EXAMPLE 3: LEFT KNEE, SECONDARY TO RIGHT KNEE		INJURED LEFT KNEE WHEN BRACE ON RIGHT KNE FAILED	6/11/2008

FIGURE 3: VA FORM 21-526EZ - SECTION V: CLAIM INFORMATION

Each example on the form pictured above shows how the condition is service-connected. Example 1 is hearing loss caused by the veteran's job (MOS), which is Direct Service Connection. Example 2 is diabetes, which is listed as an illness caused by Agent Orange exposure, and the date listed meets the requirement for Presumptive Service Connection according to the criteria. In Example 3, the veteran is claiming Secondary Service Connection because a condition already service connected (right knee) caused a secondary condition (left knee).

This section only allows you to provide enough information that fills the boxes and no more (the boxes do not expand), so be as succinct and direct as possible. You can elaborate more during your medical exam(s), in the appropriate supplementary forms (more on supplementary forms below), and by submitting the appropriate STRs and evidence as discussed previously.

This is why I encourage veterans to use **VA Form 21-4138** "Statement in Support of Claim" *along with* VA Form 21-526EZ because it allows more space to write. It also allows someone else to make statements on your behalf if they have firsthand knowledge of your condition, known as a "buddy statement" or "lay statement."

Too much information may confuse the rater as to why you're claiming your specific medical issue(s). You don't need to tell the rater all the distinct details. However, it's good to give more information than allowed on VA Form 21-526EZ.

A good example of what to write would be something like: "I'm claiming a right knee condition with pain and pain on reduced range of motion. I was treated in service several times, and since my discharge, I continue to have right knee pain with pain on reduced range of motion."

In that short example, I'm telling the VA rater four things: 1) what condition I'm claiming: "right knee condition"; 2) what symptoms I'm having: "pain and pain on reduced range of motion"; 3) how this condition is connected to my service under the five ways of service connection: "I was treated in service several times" (Direct Service Connection); and 4) that my symptoms have continued since my service: "since my service, I continue to have right knee pain…"

And here's a tip: because the wording states I have "pain," the VA can use that as subjective evidence even if there is no mention of "pain" in your C&P exam (under 38CFR 4.59).

Another example would be: "I am claiming PTSD due to fear of hostile military terrorist activity while serving in Iraq. Please review my DD214, which shows service in SWA." (SWA stands for Southwest Asia.) That may seem simple, but sometimes, depending on your claim, this is all you need.

It's important to remember the military motto: "Keep it simple, stupid." The VA employees who look at your claim are not doctors. Sometimes the more information you write on the forms and the more evidence you submit, the more they get overwhelmed and request additional information or evidence, which can cause indefinite delays to your claim (and automatically turns your fully developed claim into a Standard Claim).

The specifics of your condition(s) should be explained in detail when you meet with an examiner during your C&P exam. Therefore, make the VA's job simple and easy, and leave the medical opinions to the medical examiners. The VA raters need to know what you're claiming, how it's related to your service, the symptoms you're having (especially according to the diagnostic codes and percentages as covered earlier), and that it's still an issue after your service.

Make sure you write your social security number at the top of every page on each claim form you're using. Fill out each block as appropriate. Print the forms you're using, carefully review them with fresh eyes, sign and date them, then scan them onto your computer or device. Save them with appropriate names (such as "Lastname_21-526EZ") along with any evidence you want to submit. Now you're ready to upload your signed forms and any evidence using QuickSubmit.

KMD89'S TOP 5 MOST COMMON SERVICE-CONNECTED CLAIMS

Below are the five claims I've seen most often as a VA rater and consultant, including an overview of how to claim each if they apply to you.

1. SLEEP APNEA

Sleep Apnea is one of the main conditions veterans try to claim. In most cases, it isn't listed in their active-duty medical records because they didn't get a sleep study done while on active duty. A sleep study is now a VA requirement to qualify for service connection. You can learn more by reading 38 CFR 4.97, Diagnostic Code 6847.

So, if you're still on active duty and think you may have sleep apnea, definitely get it checked now before you separate or retire.

If you had a confirmed diagnosis of sleep apnea from a sleep study and were given a CPAP machine while on active duty, that is a 50% disability rating (though this could change, so keep updated on the regulation). However, if you were not diagnosed while on active duty, even if you were diagnosed by a VA Medical Center (VAMC), service connection will be much harder to prove, and will most likely be denied under the current criteria (for Direct

Service Connection). The VA proposed to make changes to the sleep apnea diagnostic code criteria in 2022, but the proposed changes have not been made as of the time of writing this book."

2. TINNITUS

Tinnitus (ringing in the ears) is caused by being exposed to acoustic trauma, such as (but not limited to) combat, working in a maintenance bay, working on a flight deck or flight line (or close to it), and/or being a pilot. (Though getting it diagnosed while on active duty if you have it will increase your chances of being granted service connection, especially if you don't have an MOS that would normally cause acoustic trauma.)

As of this writing (and subject to change), tinnitus is one of the easier claims to make because if you were treated in service, you shouldn't need a medical opinion—that was one of my first mistakes as an RSVR. A veteran filed a claim for tinnitus and went to a C&P exam, but the C&P examiner gave a negative opinion, so I denied the claim. When I was told of the error, I realized that his STRs showed he was seen in service for tinnitus, therefore he was eligible for tinnitus service connection regardless of the C&P examiner's decision. So, I fixed the error and granted the veteran the compensation benefit for tinnitus.

Tinnitus is a 10% disability rating currently. However, the VA proposed to remove tinnitus from their rating schedule and **combine it with hearing loss** in 2022. At the time of this writing, those proposed changes have not been made. Read M21-1 V.iii.2.B.3. – Conditions of the Auditory System to learn more, and check for any updates prior to submitting your claim.

3. MIGRAINES

Migraines is another claim that is easy to receive benefits for if it's documented in your STRs. To learn more, review 38 CFR 4.124a and M21-1 V.iii.12.A.3.

It's good to keep a log of how often you get migraines and how severe they are. There are apps you can download on your phone to help you keep track of your migraines. All that information can be presented to a C&P examiner to help prove your case. If migraines interfere with your employment, it can be up to a 50% disability rating.

4. JOINT PAIN

Years of ground and pound take a toll on the body, so report any joint pain when you first feel it (especially when you're still on active duty), then report it if it continues or gets worse. Joint pain includes pain in the ankles, knees, hips, back, neck, shoulders, elbows, and wrists. Being awarded the parachute badge is a good way to prove service connection for joint pain. Consult 38 CFR 4.71a "Schedule of ratings – musculoskeletal system."

5. PTSD

Post-Traumatic Stress Disorder (PTSD) is defined in M21-1 VIII.iv.1.A.1.a. as a psychiatric disorder that may occur in people who have experienced or witnessed a traumatic event, also known as a "stressor." M21-1 VIII. iv.1.A.1.b. defines a stressor as a "traumatic event (or series of events) in which an individual has been personally or indirectly exposed to actual or threatened death, serious injury, or sexual violence."

VA Form 21-526EZ states you also need to submit **VA Form 21-0781** or **VA Form 21-0781a** if you're claiming PTSD; however, this is not necessary in all cases. It depends on how you're claiming PTSD.

"Combat PTSD" is caused by experiencing fear of hostile military or terrorist activity and/or by engaging in combat with an enemy force. Combat PTSD is usually fairly easy to claim as a service connection. If your DD214 shows that you served in one or more hostile locations or combat zones, that is often enough to warrant a C&P exam. During the C&P exam, the examiner should confirm your PTSD symptoms, their severity, and the details that caused it.

There are several *combat zones* listed in the 38 CFR and the M21-1, including Afghanistan, Iraq, Vietnam, Kuwait, Saudi Arabia, UAE, Bahrain, Qatar, the Persian Gulf, and more. Check the regulations to see all the locations, especially for the Gulf War and Vietnam, which are always being updated (for example, see 38 CFR 3.317 – "Compensation for certain disabilities occurring in Persian Gulf veterans"). If for some reason a location you served at is not listed on your DD214, or you want to submit further evidence, you can use any official documentation that states your name and specific location. Some examples include an award write-up or a certificate.

Several areas are listed as combat locations because they were contaminated by Agent Orange during certain time periods. The criteria differ for each area. Not all areas are listed in the regulations. Currently the areas listed are: Vietnam – 38 CFR 3.313; Korea – M21-1 VIII.i.1.A.3.; Thailand – M21-1 VIII.i.1.A.4.; Johnston Island – M21-1 VIII.i.1.A.5.; Laos – M21-1 V111.i.1.A.6.a.; Cambodia – M21-1 V111.i.1.B.1.d. (at Mimot or Krek, Kampong Cham Province); and Guam or American Samoa or in the territorial waters of Guam or American Samoa (from January 9, 1962 through July 31, 1980). To learn more, search "PACT Act" on the VA's website, then scroll down and click on "Vietnam era Veteran eligibility."

If you *engaged in combat with an enemy force*, you could also use documentation of a Combat Action Badge (CAB), Combat Infantryman Badge (CIB), and/or Combat Medical Badge (CMB) (Army); Combat Action Ribbon (CAR) (Navy, Marines, Coast Guard); and/or Combat Action Medal (CAM) (Air Force, Space Force), and the equivalent.

"Non-combat events" are defined in M21-1 VIII. iv.1.A.3.g. as stressor events while on active duty not caused by hostile military or terrorist activity, such as (but not limited to) natural disasters, life-threatening disease of self or significant other, duty on a burn ward, graves registration, actual or threatened death or serious injury, witnessing the death or serious injury of another person, friendly fire during a training mission, and/or a ship sinking, an explosion, or a plane crash during active duty training or other serious training accident.

The main distinction between a combat and a non-combat stressor is that the non-combat stressor must always be corroborated with credible supporting evidence. This is where (in most instances other than combat) you would need to fill out **VA Form 21-0781** "Statement in Support of Claim for Service Connection for Post-Traumatic Stress Disorder (PTSD)," and include additional evidence and/or information.

An example would be if you saw someone killed during training. On **VA Form 21-0781**, you don't need to go into every detail as this can be re-traumatizing, but you do need to state the facts as best as you can remember them. If you don't have much information to list on this form, any other supporting evidence can be helpful, such as a military document, police report, or news article that mentions the incident or person injured/killed, if you have that information. You can also use **VA Form 21-4138** "Statement in Support of Claim," which allows someone else to make statements on your behalf, known as a "buddy statement," if they have firsthand knowledge of the incident. For more information on claiming non-combat PTSD, see 38 CFR 3.304(f), and M21-1 VIII.iv.1.A.3.g. and VIII.iv.1.A.3.m.

"Personal trauma" broadly refers to stressor events while on active duty involving harm perpetrated by a person who is not considered part of an enemy force. Examples include assault, battery, robbery, mugging, stalking, harassment, and more. Personal trauma is governed by 38 CFR 3.304(f). Special criteria and considerations for personal trauma PTSD claims are provided in M21-1 VIII.iv.1.B.

When claiming personal trauma on form **VA Form 21-526EZ**, you also need to fill out **VA Form 21-0781a** "Statement in Support of Claim for Service Connection for Post-Traumatic Stress Disorder (PTSD) Secondary to Personal Assault." You *do not* have to give the VA explicit details about the trauma you experienced other than the basic documentation needed for evidence. (Keep it simple, stupid!)

"Military sexual trauma" (MST) is a subset of personal trauma defined as any sexual harassment, sexual assault, or rape that occurred in a military setting during service. MST can happen to all genders and ages, ranks, branches, and eras of service, so if it happened to you, you're not alone. KMD89 has a YouTube video: "Military Sexual Trauma (MST) VA Disability Rating Claim Explained," and another video: "Military Sexual Assault Survivor Speaks Out!"

If you have been sexually harassed and/or assaulted and you're still in the military, report it if you can (if not to the chain of command, then to a family member, Chaplin, battle buddy, etc.). However, the VA understands that many incidents of personal trauma are not officially reported, and that victims of this type of in-service trauma often find it difficult to produce evidence to support the stressor occurrence.

If there is no explicit evidence, then alternate supporting evidence may be used, sometimes called a "marker," as covered in 38 CFR 3.304(f)(5) and M21-1 VIII. iv.1.E.1.c. Examples of a "marker" of personal trauma would be evidence of behavioral changes around the time of and/or after the trauma occurred, a counseling statement showing a change in behavior, a divorce after the incident, or separation from the military not long after the incident. For example, a veteran was sexually assaulted while in the military but didn't report it because the attacker was his/her superior. However, the veteran went to sick call a few days later and requested an STD test, pregnancy test, or complained of pain in their lower abdominal area, and that visit was recorded in their STRs—that medical visit could be considered a marker. For more information on markers, go to M21-1 VIII.iv.1.E.1.d.

I've heard that some examiners think if it was only reported once, it was resolved, and you shouldn't claim it. We veterans know this is not always true. We were trained to suck it up and drive on, which means we probably didn't go to medical every time something hurt.

If you're still on active duty, you have an opportunity to fix that. If you're no longer on active duty, keep reading the regulations so you know how to prove your claim.

Unfortunately, if you don't have evidence directly from service, or evidence of a stressor event or a marker, then it may be difficult to prove your claim is service connected or that the traumatic event occurred. Sometimes the easiest mental health claim is *PTSD for service in a hostile area*, even if your condition is more complicated than that, provided you've been treated for PTSD during service or since you left the military. If you have any questions or concerns regarding your claim, KMD89 is here to educate you on the best ways forward.

CHAPTER 4 CHECKLIST

1. Familiarize yourself with the **VA Claim Form 21-526EZ**, read the instructions on the form, and determine what other forms you may need (such as **VA Form 21-0781** and/or **VA Form 21-0781a for PTSD**, or **VA Form 21-4138** for additional information or a buddy/lay statement).

2. Review "KMD89's Top 5 Most Common Service-Connected Claims" if you're planning to claim sleep apnea, tinnitus, migraines, joint pain, and/or PTSD.

You're almost there—don't give up!

SUBMITTING YOUR CLAIM

Now that you've completed the steps covered in this book according to the regulations that pertain to your particular claim, gathered any relevant evidence to support your claim, and properly filled out the correct claim form(s), you are ready to submit your claim.

CHAPTER 5 OVERVIEW

- Submit Your Claim
- Report to BDD Claim Examinations (on active duty)

- Report to C&P Examinations (as a veteran)
- Freedom of Information Act
- My Experience with Evidence and Examinations

SUBMIT YOUR CLAIM

There are different methods for submitting your claim online as well as offline (either as a veteran or when submitting a BDD claim while on active duty), which are listed below. I think the best way is Direct Upload via "AccessVA," otherwise known as "QuickSubmit." This method allows you to upload the needed form(s) and any other evidence as attachments, and it keeps those documents online for you to view at any time (though you should still keep a backup copy of everything just in case). The other online method asks you a series of questions and populates the form for you, which can be confusing since you're not filling out the actual form. It also does not keep your documents available to view. But the choice is yours, so do what you're comfortable with.

Remember if you're submitting a BDD claim (while on active duty, as covered in Chapter 2), you must be within that 180-to-90-day window before your discharge/retirement date (preferably on the 180th day from your separation date). For both service members and veterans, you can submit your claim and supporting documents and evidence in the following ways:

- QuickSubmit (AccessVA) online
  - ○ Go to VA QuickSubmit (or Direct Upload via AccessVA) or search for "QuickSubmit" on the VA's website (www.va.gov)
  - ○ Sign in with the appropriate credentials (there are several ways to login)
  - ○ Click on the blue "QuickSubmit" tab
  - ○ Double check that your name, SSN, and zip code are correct
  - ○ Attach/upload your completed **VA Form 21-526EZ** and any other required forms and/or supporting evidence (especially if you're submitting a fully developed claim)
  - ○ For a step-by-step tutorial on QuickSubmit, watch my YouTube video "VA Quick-Submit Claim - How to expedite your VA Claim to the VA"

- Or submit online via the VA's website
    - Go to www.va.gov, search "How to file a claim," scroll down to the green arrow and click on the link that says, "File a disability compensation claim online," then click on the blue link that says, "Sign in to start your application."
    - Sign in with the appropriate credentials (there are several ways to log in)
    - Fill out the information as described and submit your claim—if you cannot complete the claim form in one session, make sure to save it before logging out
- Or *mail* your completed **VA Form 21-526EZ** and supporting documents in an envelope to:

    Department of Veterans Affairs

    Evidence Intake Center

    P.O. Box 4444

    Janesville, WI 53547-4444

- Or *for BDD claims only, personally submit* your completed **VA Form 21-526EZ** and supporting documents in an envelope to your installation's intake center representative or military service coordinator

QuickSubmit is the fastest way to submit your claim. Most service members I've worked with received a notification to report to a medical exam within a few weeks (if they submitted a fully developed claim), though each claim is different.

Submitting your claim is not all you have to do. I highly recommend you always *keep a copy of all the documents you submit* for your records, no matter how you submit them. Even though the QuickSubmit option keeps your documents online, you never know when there could be a technical glitch and the VA could temporarily, or permanently, lose access to those documents.

You should also *keep a copy of all VA correspondence concerning your claim* for your records. What one VA representative says may not get communicated properly, so keeping a copy of all the letters, emails, and faxes you sent and received will be vital if any issues come up while your claim is being processed. This is especially true if you think the VA is in error when you receive your rating decision and if you decide to submit a "Decision Review Request: Higher-Level Review."

The documents you've saved may be the only proof you have of the VA's mistakes.

REPORT TO BDD CLAIM EXAMINATIONS

If you're still on active duty and are submitting a BDD claim (as discussed in Chapter 2), you must be available to report for medical examinations between 10 and 45 days from the date your claim is received, as per M21-1 X.6.B.1.a. (if needed in addition to your retirement or separation exam, depending on what you're claiming). For example: if you submit your claim on January 1, you must be available for examinations from January 10 through February 23. Though keep in mind that VA timelines for exams are not always accurate, and exams could be even further delayed if you are in a remote location.

Your exams will be scheduled at the location nearest the address you used when you filed your claim. If you're planning to move or travel during those 45 days, be careful which address you put on your claim. This is another reason to file on the 180th day because that gives you six months to finish those exams, which can be done while you're still at your regular duty station. Then you won't have to worry about exams when you're on terminal leave. You can also add a temporary address on the **VA Form 21-526EZ** if you know you'll be traveling within that 45-day period.

WHEN THE VA FAILS TO SCHEDULE EXAMS WITHIN 45 DAYS

If you are unable to attend the required examinations within the prescribed 45-day time period due to a delay on the VA's part, *do not* remove your claim from the BDD program. Do everything possible to have the examination performed prior to discharge, including requesting the appropriate examination at your current location prior to performing the actions in M21-1 X.i.6.C.1.d. and X.i.6.C.1.e.

Visit your installation's intake center representative/ military service coordinator for support if you feel the VA is not doing what they're supposed to or not doing it in a timely manner.

REPORT TO C&P EXAMINATIONS (AS A VETERAN)

As a veteran, once the VA has received your claim, a VA rater (or other VA employee) will determine if a compensation and pension (C&P) exam is needed to validate your claim and to verify the percentage of compensation you are eligible to receive. This depends on what you're claiming and what evidence you submitted with your claim.

C&P EXAMINATIONS

If a C&P exam is needed, it may take place with a VA Healthcare C&P examiner, or more commonly with a VA-approved third-party examiner (at no cost to you), so don't be surprised if your C&P exam is not at the VA.

The form the VA uses for all C&P exams is called the "Disability Benefits Questionnaire" (DBQ). There are different DBQs for different types of conditions. Looking at the relevant DBQs ahead of your appointment can really help you prepare for your exams, so you'll know exactly what the examiner is looking for. Search for "DBQ" on the VA's website and click on the page titled "Disability Benefits Questionnaires (DBQs)," which has all the DBQs available for download.

If you're claiming multiple conditions that fall under different categories, you may require more than one C&P exam, because each C&P exam uses a different DBQ. For example, say you're claiming hearing loss, traumatic brain injury (TBI), and post-traumatic stress disorder (PTSD). Hearing loss falls under the category of auditory impairment, TBI falls under neurological conditions, and PTSD falls under mental disorders. Most likely, you'll need three different C&P exams with three different specialists. A general practitioner won't be able to evaluate all three conditions. And if one examiner can evaluate all the conditions you're claiming, they'll still need different DBQs if they're evaluating conditions that fall under different categories.

Once the VA's C&P office or third-party contractor's office calls to schedule or confirm your C&P exams, ask them what conditions you're reporting for. This helps ensure you're being evaluated for all the conditions you've claimed (that fall under the five ways of service connection). You can also call the VA benefits hotline (VA national call center) at 1-800-827-1000 and ask them what exams or DBQs are on the exam request, known as a 2507 "Request for Physical Examination." If you still don't have the answers, ask the examiner when you arrive at your C&P exam(s).

Since you're educated on your conditions and your eligible rating percentages, and you've been to the VA's website and downloaded and reviewed the DBQ for each condition you have, you should know how to use the VA's medical language to communicate your conditions, symptoms, and effects on your life to the examiner. You want minimal confusion and cause for error.

For example, if you have a back injury that falls under diagnostic code 5237: lumbosacral or cervical strain, a spine condition rated under "General Rating Formula for Diseases and Injuries of the Spine" as per 38 CFR 4.71a, you will see the rating percentages and criteria, as listed below.

- With or without symptoms such as pain (whether or not it radiates), stiffness, or aching in the area of the spine affected by residuals of injury or disease
  - Unfavorable ankylosis of the entire spine 100
  - Unfavorable ankylosis of the entire thoracolumbar spine 50
  - Unfavorable ankylosis of the entire cervical spine; or, **forward flexion of the thoracolumbar spine 30 degrees or less**; or, favorable ankylosis of the entire thoracolumbar spine. 40
  - **Forward flexion of the cervical spine 15 degrees or less**; or, favorable ankylosis of the entire cervical spine. 30
  - **Forward flexion of the thoracolumbar spine greater than 30 degrees but not greater than 60 degrees**; or, **forward flexion of the cervical spine greater than 15 degrees** but not greater than 30 degrees; or, the combined range of motion of the thoracolumbar spine not greater than 120 degrees; or, the combined range of motion of the cervical spine not greater than 170 degrees; or, muscle spasm or guarding severe enough to result in an abnormal gait or abnormal spinal contour such as scoliosis, reversed lordosis, or abnormal kyphosis. . . 20

○ **Forward flexion of the thoracolumbar spine greater than 60 degrees but not greater than 85 degrees**; or, **forward flexion of the cervical spine greater than 30 degrees but not greater than 40 degrees**; or, combined range of motion of the thoracolumbar spine greater than 120 degrees but not greater than 235 degrees; or, combined range of motion of the cervical spine greater than 170 degrees but not greater than 335 degrees; or, muscle spasm, guarding, or localized tenderness not resulting in abnormal gait or abnormal spinal contour; or, vertebral body fracture with loss of 50 percent or more of the height. 10

I have highlighted in bold the range of motion, which is a main criterion for how a lumbosacral or cervical spine condition is rated. The 38 CFR even provides diagrams showing exactly what the medical examiner should look for, as shown on the next page.

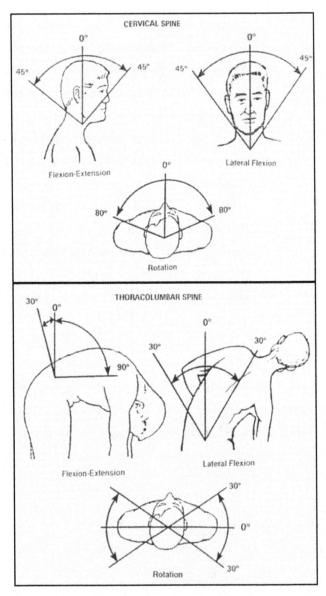

FIGURE 4: RANGE OF MOTION DIAGRAMS FOR DIAGNOSTIC CODE 5237:
LUMBOSACRAL OR CERVICAL STRAIN

These criteria are reflected on the DBQ the examiner fills out during your exam. While the DBQ for back injuries is lengthy, below shows a section where the examiner will annotate your condition similar to the rating criteria.

Active Range of Motion (ROM) - Perform active range of motion and provide the ROM values:

Forward flexion endpoint (90 degrees): _____ degrees   Left lateral flexion endpoint (30 degrees): _____ degrees

Extention endpoint (30 degrees): _____ degrees   Right lateral rotation endpoint (30 degrees): _____ degrees

Right lateral flexion endpoint (30 degrees): _____ degrees   Left lateral rotation endpoint (30 degrees): _____ degrees

If noted on examination, which ROM exhibited pain (select all that apply):

☐ Forward flextion   ☐ Right lateral flexion   ☐ Right lateral Rotation

☐ Extention   ☐ Light lateral flexion   ☐ Left lateral Rotation

If any limitation of motion is specifically attributed to pain, weakness, fatigability, incoordination, or other; please note the gegree(s)in which limitation of motion is specifically attributed to the factors identified and describe.

Forward flexion: _____ Degree endpoint (if different than above)   Left lateral flexion: _____ Degree endpoint (if different than above)

Extention: _____ Degree endpoint (if different than above)   Right lateral rotation: _____ Degree endpoint (if different than above)

Right lateral flexion: _____ Degree endpoint (if different than above)   Left lateral rotation: _____ Degree endpoint (if different than above)

FIGURE 5: BACK (THORACOLUMBAR SPINE) CONDITIONS
DISABILITY BENEFITS QUESTIONNAIRE (DBQ)

Knowing the five ways of service connection and diagnostic code criteria for your conditions will greatly help you prepare for your C&P exam. Understanding the Disability Benefits Questionnaire (DBQ) for each condition you're claiming will help as well. You can use a separate 3x5 notecard for each condition, noting all your symptoms for that condition. Bring them to your exam so you remember to mention all the symptoms the examiner will be looking for. Doing this will help prevent miscommunication and possible complications in your claim's journey.

As I've said, not all examiners are advocates for veterans. When I went to my C&P exam for lower back pain, the first thing the examiner told me was to take off my shoes. As you know, a determining factor for a lot of physical (musculoskeletal) conditions is range of motion (in this case, forward flexion/leaning forward). By simply watching to see if I bent over to remove my shoes, the examiner hoped to determine my range of motion and pain level without me even knowing it. But I was wearing sandals and slipped them off with my feet, without bending over. That forced the examiner to conduct the proper exam.

Examiners may try to ask questions and talk about issues that are outside your military service so they can deny you service connection, including in mental health exams (for instance, to determine if you had a mental illness or an event that affected you more than your military experience did). So it's important to be prepared, do your research, and stay on topic. Focus on what happened during your active-duty service, and how your conditions have impacted you and/or worsened since service (if you are no longer on active duty).

Don't hold back. Be honest.

ISSUES WITH SCHEDULING

While most VA-directed C&P exams are now scheduled with third-party contractors, if you prefer to be seen at a VA C&P facility, you can request a VA C&P examiner instead of a third-party examiner.

PUBLIC DBQS

As mentioned in Chapter 3, you can have a provider of your choice complete your C&P exam at your own cost, which is commonly called a "public DBQ exam" or just "DBQ." Keep in mind, you will *not* be reimbursed for the cost. And, you will need to complete the public DBQ exam *prior to submitting your claim*, so that you can submit the DBQ paperwork (and Nexus Statement if needed) at the same time you submit your claim form(s) and any other evidence as needed.

Unfortunately, I've seen some veterans' public DBQs get rejected for no reason, and the VA is still scheduling C&P exams for the same conditions. A few of those veterans refused to attend the VA-directed C&P exam because they knew their public DBQs were actionable and sufficient, and they didn't want conflicting medical evidence in their claim. In those situations, contact the VA and ask them why they are scheduling a C&P exam instead of using the DBQ as sufficient evidence. 38 CFR 3.159(c)(4)(i) "Department of Veterans Affairs assistance in developing claims" clearly states that if the DBQ is actionable and sufficient, meaning the proper DBQ (and Nexus Letter, if required) was completed per VA guidelines by a verifiable healthcare provider, the VA should use the DBQ instead of a VA-directed C&P exam. The representatives at the VA call center may not know why an exam was requested, but it will be noted in your claim file that you called in and questioned this action.

Call the VA benefits hotline/VA national call center at 1-800-827-1000. If they are not helpful, you can file a complaint with the White House VA Hotline at 1-855-948-2311 and request a call back from the Veterans Benefits Administration (VBA) (preferably from a supervisor). You can opt to receive an email, but then you may not get a complete answer to your question.

If the VA denies your claim for not reporting to a VA-directed C&P exam when you know you submitted an actionable and sufficient DBQ, you have options. The notification letter you receive in your rating decision packet will outline these options, including a Supplemental Claim, Higher-Level Review, and Board of Veterans' Appeals (BVA). (These options and the notification letter are covered in Chapter 6.)

I've seen many veterans who had to fight to have their public DBQs and Nexus Letters accepted, so knowing the VA guidelines on public DBQs (and ensuring the private provider knows the guidelines) is key. It's up to the veteran to ensure the DBQ is actionable and sufficient for rating purposes. The VA has many regulations on public DBQ exams, and I've provided several YouTube videos on this topic as well. KMD89 will also review your DBQ and Nexus Letters to ensure they're actionable and sufficient before you submit them. And we offer classes that go over DBQs and Nexus Statements with examples.

FREEDOM OF INFORMATION ACT

If you had a bad experience during a VA-directed C&P examination, or you were denied benefits and are unsure why, you can submit a Privacy Act (PA) Request or Freedom of Information Act (FOIA) Request to obtain a copy of your VA-directed C&P exam and entire Veterans Benefits Administration (VBA) claims folder. It may take a few weeks or even months before you receive a copy, but it will allow you to see everything the examiner wrote. It's important to know *you are entitled to a copy of your exams*. Even if you received a positive decision, it's still a good idea to have a copy of your examiner's notes in your own records. It's especially important to request a copy if you received an unfavorable rating decision. You want to understand the reason for denial or lower percentage.

If you had the C&P exam at the VA, it should also be in your VA progress notes in your "My HealtheVet" account.

Sometimes a claim is easy, other times it's not. Unfortunately, it really depends on the VA rater and/or C&P examiner you have. It shouldn't be that way, but some people think it's a welfare system when it's not. So, keep copies of everything you send and receive from the VA, just in case. You can also watch my YouTube video "How to obtain a copy of your VA rating decision and other documents from the VA website."

MY EXPERIENCE WITH EVIDENCE AND EXAMINATIONS

When I went to my first C&P exam, I found out the examiner wasn't evaluating me for all the conditions I was claiming. He said, "This is all the information I have from the regional office." So, I was approved for some conditions, but the VA denied the rest because they said I hadn't been treated in service for those things. But I knew I had been. I also knew that 38 CFR 3.304 and 3.305 state if you had an injury, made a complaint, were given a diagnosis, and/or were treated for something, you should get a C&P exam for that condition.

After submitting a FOIA request for my STRs, I looked through my medical records, saw those other conditions, and filed a re-open claim (now called a supplemental claim). I also submitted the new and material evidence (now called new and relevant evidence). I eventually had four different VA C&P exams. Two of those examiners were really professional; they took the time to listen to me and document what we discussed. But the other two examiners didn't seem to care; one even made rude comments during the exam.

After obtaining a copy of my VA C&P exams through the Release of Information Office at the VA, I found out the two examiners I hadn't been comfortable with had not filled out the exam accurately. Neither examiner asked me the specific questions they should have asked about my conditions. One examiner even outright lied, stating he'd asked me certain questions and that I'd responded a certain way—yet he'd *never* asked these questions, and I obviously had not responded! I then knew I needed to redo those exams with different providers.

I sent a letter to the director of the VA medical center where I'd had the worst C&P exam. I filed a formal complaint against that examiner. The VA said they were looking into it, but in the meantime, I should appeal the rating decision. I was adamant I shouldn't have to appeal, and I requested a new C&P exam. Finally, about six months later, I got another C&P exam with a different examiner. And that time it was a positive experience.

Once the VA allowed the option of public DBQs, I made the decision to have my own private doctors complete my C&P exams from then on. I based this decision on my experiences with the two horrible C&P examiners. After I submitted my last DBQ, a third-party examiner's office called me and stated they needed to schedule me for a C&P exam. I informed them I would not be attending the exam because I knew my public DBQ was actionable and sufficient per VA regulations. I didn't want any possibility of conflicting medical evidence. Fortunately, about two weeks later, the VA rater agreed, and I received a positive rating decision.

I certainly hope you don't go through everything I did, but this is why educating yourself on your claim is so important. You never know what might happen.

CHAPTER 5 CHECKLIST

1. Submit your claim using the proper forms and supporting evidence as applicable.
2. Research the DBQs for the conditions you're claiming and report to your medical exams as needed.

3. Keep copies of all your claim documents and correspondence to and from the VA for your records.
4. Use the Privacy Act (PA) or Freedom of Information Act (FOIA) to request a copy of your VA-directed C&P exam(s).
5. Don't quit!

YOUR RATING
DECISION &
NEXT STEPS

After you've submitted your claim and attended any needed medical examinations, you should receive your notification letter and rating decision. This chapter will cover what to expect, how to interpret your rating decision, and what to do if you are denied or receive less of a percentage than you think you're eligible for.

CHAPTER 6 OVERVIEW

- Important Forms & Letters
- How the VA Determines Your Overall Disability Percentage
- Step 1: Wait
- Step 2: Request a Copy of Your VA Claims Folder
- Step 3: Understand Your Notification Letter and Rating Decision Letter
  - I have a YouTube video "Difference between VA Claim Notification Letter and Rating Decision"
- Step 4: Request Your Disability Breakdown Letter
- Next Steps
- Increase Claim
- Supplemental Claim
- Higher-Level Review
- Board of Veterans' Appeal
- My Experience with Mistakes & Appeals
- Final Thoughts

IMPORTANT FORMS & LETTERS

- Notification Letter
  - o This is one of two letters included in the rating decision packet you receive from the VA.
  - o It covers your overall rating decision, payment information, dependent payments, what to do if you disagree, additional benefits, and more.
- Rating Decision Letter
  - o This is the second letter included in the packet.
  - o It details how the VA made their decision and what evidence they used.
- Disability Breakdown Letter
  - o This is *not* included with your notification letter and rating decision—you have to request it from the VA.
  - o It details the conditions you were approved for with the exact diagnostic codes and rating percentages.
  - o If you are service connected, you can obtain this letter by calling 1-800-827-1000 and asking for a "disability breakdown letter to

include the diagnostic codes." Request they email it to you.

- o Watch my YouTube video "What Evidence the VA does not send you with your Rating Decision: Code Sheet"

- **VA Form 20-0995** "Decision Review Request: Supplemental Claim"

  - o If you were denied for service connection on a previous claim, you can submit a supplemental claim.

  - o This essentially reconsiders or re-opens that previous claim and allows you to provide new and relevant evidence to support it.

- **VA Form 20-0996** "Decision Review Request: Higher-Level Review"

  - o A higher-level review is previously known as an "appeal."

  - o It is used when you feel the VA is in error (new evidence can be submitted but will *not* be considered).

- **VA Form 10182** "Decision Review Request: Board Appeal (Notice of Disagreement)"

  - o A Board Appeal is used when you appeal a VA decision to a Veterans Law Judge located at the Board of Veterans' Appeals in Washington, D.C. (You do not have to travel to Washington, D.C. to use this method; there are various options listed on the form.)

HOW THE VA DETERMINES YOUR OVERALL DISABILITY PERCENTAGE

The way the VA will determine your overall percentage of disability compensation is quite complicated, so I'll only cover this briefly.

If you claimed more than one condition, it's good to check if those conditions fall under the same or different rating categories. This is based on the diagnostic criteria and rating percentages as described in Chapter 1.

For instance, if you suffer from both PTSD (post-traumatic stress disorder) and panic attacks (panic disorder), they both fall under the "General Rating Formula for Mental Disorders" as per 38 CFR 4.125. In that case, you would look at how both of those conditions affect your overall mental health rating. You can't be service connected for PTSD at 50% and panic disorder at 30% to get a total of 80% disability. That would be an example of "pyramiding," as per 38 CFR 4.14 ("Avoidance of pyramiding.")

Now, for someone who is suffering from both PTSD and panic disorder, that may not seem fair. But to the VA, mental is mental.

If you have conditions that fall in different rating categories, the total for each rating category will be added together to determine your overall disability rating; but it's not regular math, it's VA math. You have to know how to do the VA math, or look at a VA rating calculator or table. You can find the rating table in 38CFR 4.25 "Combined ratings table."

For example, if you have a left knee replacement at 60% (severe pain), migraines at 30%, and tinnitus at 10% (three different rating categories), the VA math wouldn't add up to 100%. Instead, the combined total disability rating would equal 78%, which would then be rounded up to 80%.

Why the VA does its math this way, I can't tell you. What's important to understand is *how* rating percentages are combined to better understand your rating decision when you receive it. Check out the table in the 38 CFR ahead of time so you know what to expect.

The maximum compensation you can receive is 100%. But veterans can receive additional compensation benefits if they qualify for **special monthly compensation (SMC)** due to certain needs or disabilities. The VA defines "special monthly compensation/SMC" as additional compensation above the basic levels of compensation—based on a disability rating of 0% to 100% for various types of anatomical losses or levels of impairment due solely to service-connected disabilities. You can learn more at https://benefits. va.gov, click on the "Compensation" drop-down menu on the left, then click on "Types of Compensation." You can also review 38CFR 3.350 and M21-1 VIII.iv.4.A. – Special Monthly Compensation (SMC).

Veterans can also receive benefits listed under **permanent and total (P&T)** disability and **individual unemployability (IU)** as per 38 CFR 3.340, 4.16, and 6.18. I won't go into depth on SMC, P&T, or IU in this book, but if you (or a family member) have one or more service-connected disabilities that require special care or prevent you from gainful employment, there are additional benefits you may qualify for. KMD89 VA Claims Consulting® works with all ranges of disability and VA compensation benefits if you (or a loved one) would like more education in this area.

STEP 1:
WAIT

Waiting is key. In the military, you probably experienced a lot of hurry-up-and-wait. The claims process is no different. But if you receive a favorable rating decision, you'll begin receiving a monthly, tax-free compensation benefit for the rest of your life. You may even receive an additional lump sum for back pay, especially if you did an Intent to File as I mentioned in Chapter 3. So, while you may be anxious and frustrated, know that the wait is worth it.

No guaranteed schedule is given for the amount of time it will take the VA to process your claim, and each claim is different. I've seen some veterans with presumptive claims receive their rating decision (and monthly compensation) only a few weeks after they filed their claim. Others who had to submit multiple claims with new evidence and attend multiple exams had to wait years, as I had to, before they were compensated for everything they were eligible for. Hopefully, with what you learn in this book, you'll receive your decision in a few months or less.

There are many variables to this process. In my opinion, the number one variable is the VA's current backlog. The VA has come a long way over the years and made several process improvements to help eliminate wait times, but they still have much work to do. If you choose a public DBQ and know what makes a DBQ (and Nexus Statement) actionable and sufficient, the VA rater is more likely to use the evidence to adjudicate your claim without requesting a C&P exam. This helps lower the backlog and your overall wait time for a decision.

STEP 2:
REQUEST A COPY OF YOUR
VA CLAIMS FOLDER

While you're waiting for your rating decision, I encourage you to request a copy of your entire *VA claims folder* (also, known as a c-file). While you should already have a copy of everything for your own records, requesting a copy from the VA will give you all the information that the Veterans Benefits Administration (VBA) has in your VA claims e-folder (digital file).

Like requesting a copy of your STRs, you can request a copy of your entire claims folder from the VBA using the Freedom of Information Act (FOIA) or Privacy Act (PA) using **VA Form 20-10206** "Freedom of Information Act (FOIA) or Privacy Act (PA) Request," which you can search for and download on the VA's website. Fill it out completely according to the instructions, and send it using QuickSubmit (AccessVA), or fax or mail it according to the instructions on the form. (Use the same fax number and address as previously listed for all VBA correspondence.)

It may take a few months to obtain this information. I waited eleven months to receive mine. Some veterans received a copy of their VA claims folder (c-file) in as little as two months, others up to a year. Because it usually takes a while for a FOIA/PA request to be processed, you can make your FOIA request even before you receive a rating decision.

Another option is to go to va.gov and select "Check your claim or appeal status" under the disability tab, sign in, then follow the links to download previous correspondence from the VA. You can view all VA-generated correspondence in your claims file and download those documents as PDF files. Though this is not a substitute for keeping copies of everything yourself, it's a good way to know what the VA has on record. Your claim status *should* be updated regularly, but it may not be. Check it later if you don't see everything you think should be there.

When you receive the copy of your claims folder, go through all the information. All VA-directed C&P exam information should be included, though this information may not be available until a few weeks or more after the exam. If the information isn't in your VA claims folder, and it's been more than a few months since your C&P exams, you can submit another request.

While you wait for your rating decision, you can also go to the KMD89 VA Claims Consulting® YouTube channel, Facebook page, LinkedIn page, and website, watch videos, attend our monthly Q&A sessions and our monthly veteran roundtable discussions, join our VA Disability Service Connection Facebook group, and more (all these links are listed at the end of this book under "Stay Connected with KMD89 VA Claims Consulting®").

STEP 3:
UNDERSTAND YOUR NOTIFICATION LETTER AND RATING DECISION LETTER

When you receive the VA packet in the mail with your rating decision, if you felt like I did, your heart will be pounding with anticipation and excitement. When you open the envelope, you should find two separate documents. One is the notification letter; the other is the rating decision letter.

- The notification letter (example on next page) will include the date it was written, your name and address, and:
    - Your benefit information (what they decided)
    - VA contact information (their phone number, where you can send questions, and how to obtain representation if you want it)

EXAMPLE ONLY

July 18, 2022
John Doe
000 USA Drive
Hometown, USA 00000

We have included with this letter:
1. Explanation of Payment
2. Additional Benefits
3. Where to send Your
   Correspondence
4. Rating Decision
5. Fraud Prevention

We made a decision on your VA benefits.

Attachment
Dear John Doe

This letter will guide you through the information you should know and steps you may take now that VA has made a decision about your benefits.

You requested that we expedite your claim under the FDC Program; however, we could not process your claim under this program because we received evidence after the claim was received. Because your claim was not eligible for processing under the FDC Program, we processed it under our standard claims-processing procedures.

Your Benefit Information:
- Service Connection for PTSD (claimed as anxiety, nightmares, and sleep disturbance) is granted with an evaluation of 100 percent effective May 15, 2021.
- Service connection for Tinnitus is granted with an evaluation of 10 percent is effective May 15, 2021
- Service connection for sleep apnea secondary to your claimed PTSD is denied.

Your combined rating evaluation is 100%

HOW VA Combines Percentages
If you have more than one condition, VA will combine percentages to determine your overall disability rating. The percentages assigned for each of your conditions may not always add up to your combined rating evaluation. The following website has additional information about how VA combines percentages:
http://www.beneftis.va.gov/compensation/rates-index.asp#howcalc.

Your monthly entitlement amount is shown below:

Monthly Entitlement Amount	Payment Start Date	Reason
$3,146.42 [example amount]	June 1, 2021	Original Award

We are currently paying you as a single Veteran with no dependents.

FIGURE 6: NOTIFICATION LETTER EXAMPLE (FIRST PAGE ONLY)

- o The process you should follow if you dis-
    agree with the decision they provided, in-
    cluding the name and number of the forms
    you will need
- o Additional benefits
- o The location of where to send any corre-
    spondence you may have
- o Your rights, and more
- The rating decision letter (example on next page)
  will include some of the following:
    - o Veteran's name and social security number
    - o Introduction
    - o Decision
    - o Evidence
    - o Reason for Decision

It's easy to skim over these letters and attachments, especially if you're excited or upset about the VA's decision. When you're calm, take the time to read everything fully—they provide a lot of helpful information, including why you were granted or denied benefits, why the effective date was assigned, the percentage assigned if service connected, and why that percentage was granted.

EXAMPLE ONLY

DEPARTMENT OF VETERANS AFFAIRS
Veterans Benefits Administration
Regional Office

John Doe
VA File Number
000-00-000

Rating Decision **dated**
July 15, 2022

INTRODUCTION

The records reflect that you are a Veteran of the Gulf war Era. You service in the Army from July 18, 2005 to August July 25, 2015.You filed an original disability claim that was received on May 15, 2021. Based on review of the evidence listed below, we have made the following decision on your claim.

DECISION

1. Service Connection for PTSD (claimed as anxiety, nightmares, and sleep disturbance) is granted with an evaluation of 100 percent effective May 15, 2021.
2. Service connection for Tinnitus is granted with an evaluation of 10 percent is effective May 15, 2021
3. Service connection for sleep apnea secondary to your claimed PTSD is denied.

EVIDENCE

- ☐ DD Form 214 – Certificate of Release or Discharge from Active Duty
- ☐ Service treatment records covering periods from July 18, 2005 to July 25, 2015
- ☐ VA Form 21-526EZ Veteran's Fully Developed Claim, Received May 15, 2021

FIGURE 7: RATING DECISION LETTER EXAMPLE (FIRST PAGE ONLY)

STEP 4:
REQUEST YOUR DISABILITY
BREAKDOWN LETTER

If you received a favorable rating decision, you'll now get a VA disability compensation benefit, tax-free, every month, for the rest of your life. Congratulations—you deserve it!

Unless one or more of your conditions worsens, you develop a new condition, or you need to add or remove dependents, you probably won't need to submit any other claims. (To add dependents, you must be service connected at least 30%.)

If your rating decision is not favorable, don't worry— this is not the end of the road.

If you have been granted benefits of any amount, always request a *Disability Breakdown Letter* to include the diagnostic codes. This letter will list each of your VA-approved, service-connected conditions by name, corresponding diagnostic codes, and rating percentage assigned. It also allows you to cross-reference your approved conditions with a copy of your C&P exam(s) and the criteria in the 38 CFR. This helps you determine if you need to file for an Increase Claim, Secondary Claim, or take additional steps if you feel the VA is in error.

While this letter is especially helpful if you plan to fight the VA's decision, it's good to have in your records for your knowledge and for reference if anything changes in the future.

To request this letter, call the VA benefits hotline/ VA national call center: **1-800-827-1000**. Tell the VA representative, "I would like a disability breakdown letter to include the diagnostic codes. And I would like it emailed to me." You can also have it faxed or sent by mail. (It would be helpful if the VA sent this with your rating decision and notification letters, but for whatever reason, you must request it.)

If the VA representative doesn't understand your request, or they say they're unable to email it to you, kindly hang up. Call again and talk with a different representative. Sometimes it just depends on whom you talk to.

Any time you talk to a VA employee regarding your claim, I encourage you to get their name (they will probably give you only their first name for security), their job title, and what regional office they're assigned to. Since each employee may handle your claim differently and no one is perfect, it's important to keep track of the information you receive and who gave it to you. This way, if another VA employee asks you, "Who told you that?" you'll be able to back up the information.

Below is an example of a Disability Breakdown Letter.

EXAMPLE ONLY (Disability Breakdown Letter)/Only if the veteran is serivce connected.

VA LOGO	**Department of Veteran Affairs** **000 USA Ave.** **Hometown, US 00000**

June 1, 2020   In Reply Refer To:

John Doe   000/NCC/JD
00000 Star Dr.   CSS XXXXX0000
Hometown, US 00000   Doe, J

Dear John Doe,

This is in reply to your request for a statement verifying your service connected disabilities.

Department of Veterans Affaires (VA) records show your serice-connected disability are as follows:

Percentage	Disability	Diag Code
30	Cluster and migraine headaches	8100
50	PTSD	9411
0	Lumbar strain	5237
10	Right knee strain	5260
0	Scar, right forearm	7805
0	Bilateral hearing loss	6100

70	**Combined Rating**

FIGURE 8: DISABILITY BREAKDOWN LETTER EXAMPLE

NEXT STEPS

Just because you disagree with a rating decision doesn't mean the VA is in error, or that you need a new exam, or that you should file a Decision Review Request (Higher Level Review). First, educate yourself on the reasons you were denied or why you received a certain rating percentage. I've heard veterans say, "I've served my country, so I deserve my compensation!" But that's not how it works. Remember, *it's not what you say, it's what you can prove.*

INCREASE CLAIM

If you received a smaller percentage than you think you're eligible for, or your condition worsens and you become eligible for a higher percentage, then you can submit an Increase Claim. An Increase Claim is similar to an initial claim, and you can do an Intent to File for your Increase Claim. This will allow you to possibly receive back pay for that increase, and it allows you time to gather any new evidence or get a public DBQ completed before you submit your Increase Claim. An Increase Claim uses **VA Form 21-526EZ**, which you should be familiar with at this point. The process is similar to an initial claim, so refer back to Chapter 3 as needed.

If an Increase Claim is not adequate for your situation, you have three options. They are: 1) Supplemental Claim; 2) Higher-Level Review; and 3) Board Appeal. It's important to know what is required for each before choosing.

SUPPLEMENTAL CLAIM

If you choose to submit a **VA Form 20-0995** "Decision Review Request: Supplemental Claim," you must submit new and relevant evidence to support your claim. For example, say you filed a claim for a back condition, the VA third-party C&P examiner gave a negative opinion, and the claim was denied. You obtained a copy of your VA claims e-folder on CD, reviewed it, and you feel your C&P exam was insufficient. So, you decide to have your private physician complete an actionable and sufficient DBQ and Nexus Statement for the back condition, and this new C&P exam is positive. This is *new and relevant evidence*. It's new because it is evidence that was not considered or was not part of your claim when it was adjudicated, and it's relevant as it pertains to the back condition you had tried to claim previously.

If your claim was denied because the C&P examiner gave a negative opinion, then the process went as it should as far as the VA is concerned (if the exam was sufficient and there were no mistakes made by the VA). This is why a supplemental claim works well in these cases—you are allowed to submit new and relevant evidence, such as submitting an actionable and sufficient public DBQ (as covered in Chapter 3).

As stated previously, some VA employees don't accept public DBQs and Nexus Letters even when they're actionable and sufficient (even though they're supposed to). This is another reason to stay educated on this process. You need to know your rights as a veteran.

HIGHER-LEVEL REVIEW

Rather than submit new evidence, if you believe you followed all the steps and provided all the needed evidence to support your claim, but the VA made a mistake or is in error, you can submit **VA Form 20-0996** "Decision Review Request: Higher-Level Review." A Decision Review Officer (DRO) will review your claim.

For your Higher-Level Review to be successful (especially if you request an informal conference), you should know exactly what errors the VA made in processing your claim with the evidence to back it up. You'll need that information when you fill out **VA Form 20-0996**. *New evidence will not be considered*, so be sure to read the form's instructions.

If you plan to file a Higher-Level Review, you only have one year (365 days) to do so from when you received your notification letter, as per 38 CFR 3.2601(d), so don't wait too long to gather needed information to help you prove your case.

Keep in mind a Higher-Level Review is not only for denials for service connection, but could be for incorrect effective dates, improper percentages assigned, and more. The requirements have changed from the time this step was called an appeal. The main changes are:

- The DRO should conduct a cursory review (before the informal conference, if selected) of all the evidence that was part of your claim when it was initially adjudicated to look for errors.
- You can submit new evidence, but it will *not* be considered.
- You can request an informal conference.

If the DRO does not find any errors, they will uphold the rating decision. No changes will be made to the original rating decision. If they do find any errors, they will notify you of a duty to assist error and correct any errors or differences of opinion to ensure they give you due process. This does NOT always mean they will grant the benefit, as it depends on the error/differences and how it pertains to your claim.

For example, you initially submitted an actionable and sufficient DBQ for an increase from your private provider, and your provider completed the information per VA guidelines, but you were notified to report for a C&P exam. You decided not to go since you already had sufficient evidence to rate your claim. The RVSR denied your claim because you refused the VA-directed C&P exam. So, you submit a Higher-Level Review and state that your public DBQ was sufficient, and you didn't want there to be conflicting medical evidence by seeing some-one who never treated you. In this example, the DRO can grant the benefit based on the fact the RSVR made an error by not accepting a DBQ that was actionable and sufficient according to 38 CFR 3.159(c)(4).

Keep in mind, the DRO does not have to accept the DBQ if they determine it is not actionable and sufficient. And, unfortunately, sometimes the success of your claim depends on the individuals you're dealing with, and this leads to inconsistencies. In these cases, keep fighting. You cannot submit an additional Higher-Level Review of a

Higher-Level Review, but you can submit a Supplemental Claim or a Board of Veterans' Appeal (covered next).

Many veterans tell me they're filing a Higher-Level Review because they served their country, and their claim should be service connected, but that alone is not enough. You must understand the process and the regulations and be able to identify the VA's error or the due process that was not followed. Then you must show the error that was made and/or state the regulation that the VA did not follow, and reasonably articulate how it applies to your claim.

This may sound hard to do, but if you're educated and have a copy of your claim folder (c-file), it's very possible to win your Higher-Level Review. If you need further assistance or are feeling overwhelmed, KMD89 VA Claims Consulting® is here to educate veterans on how to understand and navigate these processes.

BOARD OF VETERANS' APPEAL

The third option is to submit **VA Form 10182** "Decision Review Request: Board Appeal (Notice of Disagreement)." A Board Appeal is used when you want a judge who is an expert on veterans' law to review your case.

Your request goes directly to a Veterans Law Judge at the Board of Veterans' Appeals in Washington, D.C.

You have three options for a Board Appeal.

1. **Direct review:** a Veterans Law Judge will review your appeal based on the evidence you've already submitted. With this option, you *cannot* submit any new evidence, and you *cannot* have a hearing.

2. **Submit new evidence:** if you want to submit new evidence for a Veterans Law Judge to review, you must submit this new evidence within 90 days from the date the Board of Veterans' Appeals received your request.

3. **Request a hearing:** if you want a hearing with a Veterans Law Judge, you can submit new evidence *at* the hearing or *up to 90 days after* the hearing. The evidence will be considered but is not necessary. The hearing can be a virtual hearing from your home, a videoconference hearing at a VA location near you, or an in-person hearing at the Board in Washington, D.C. Know that you are *not* paid or reimbursed for any travel costs. A transcription of the hearing will be added to your appeal file.

The Board of Veterans' Appeals is quite backlogged. Average wait times according to the VA's website as of this writing are *one to two years*. Because of that, this option is usually best left as a last resort. To learn more, search for "board appeal" on the VA's website.

A hearing is not a time for you to simply retell your story or complain about your claim's issues. At a hearing, you either: 1) state why the VA is in error, and/or 2) state why your new evidence should be considered and how it proves your case.

Be prepared to defend your case with the appropriate evidence, claim documents, and regulations. For example, if you feel the VA has an incorrect effective date and you have a letter or other dated document that proves an earlier effective date, the VA will need that information.

MY EXPERIENCE WITH MISTAKES AND APPEALS

I appealed my own claim (back before it was changed to a Higher-Level Review) about eight items. One was for an incorrect effective date on an Increase Claim. Because I kept all the paperwork I submitted for the increase, which had a date stamp from the VA regional office showing when they received the paperwork, I had proof of the effective date (this was also before the Intent to File was in place). After several failed attempts requesting that they review my claims folder and change the effective date, I submitted an appeal. They finally scheduled a videoconference where I was able to talk to the DRO in person (via video). She kept saying she didn't see the date stamp that I submitted. Finally, I told her exactly where to look, based on the fact I had requested a copy of my claims folder and had the same information. She located the identified date stamp, and I was granted back pay to the correct effective date.

Again, keep everything you send to the VA and everything they send you, and obtain a copy of your VA claims e-folder on CD. Without me keeping this evidence, I may have never won my Higher-Level Review and never received that back pay.

If you have requested information from the VA and have not received an answer in a reasonable amount of time, or you feel you have a legitimate complaint with the VA, you can raise your issue through the White House VA Hotline by calling 1-855-948-2311. A representative will issue you a reference number (make sure you keep this for your records) and will forward it to the VA for follow-up. I used the White House Hotline when I hadn't received my VA claims folder on CD after several months of waiting, and after I called the hotline (and my complaint was forwarded to the VA), my CD arrived a couple weeks later. While this may not solve your issue, it's a tool you can use if needed.

FINAL THOUGHTS

The internet is full of information about VA disability compensation benefits. Almost any veteran who's filed a claim will tell you how they did theirs and how you should do yours. Everyone has their own experiences, knowledge, biases, and views. When asking for advice or researching the claims process, see if the person or source you're using can cite the regulation. The regulation is the proof. And while it's good to ask for advice and get feedback, it's always best to educate yourself on your own specific claim and the regulations that pertain to it. As my grandfather said, "Once you have that knowledge, nobody can take it away from you."

If you are granted VA disability compensation benefits, unfortunately, many scammers see veterans' disability benefits as easy money. Beware of people or entities that don't have your best interests in mind.

I wrote this book to help veterans like you learn how to successfully navigate the VA disability compensation claims process and maximize the benefits you're eligible to receive. The information here is by no means comprehensive. This book would be way too long if it was. I sincerely hope it gives you the power to educate yourself on your own claim. However, if you have further questions or run into issues not covered here, contact KMD89 VA Claims Consulting®. I started the company to help veterans understand this complex information and know where to go if they have questions. And I'm here to help you as much as I can.

You served your country—it's time the country served you.

CHAPTER 6 CHECKLIST

1. Understand how the VA determines your overall disability percentage by referring to the rating table.
2. Wait patiently—there is no set time for when you will receive your rating decision.
3. Request a copy of your VA claims folder so you have everything on file. This will help you prove any VA errors.
4. Review your notification and rating decision letters so you understand the contents.

5. Request a disability breakdown letter so you can see exactly what you're approved for, at what percentages, and the diagnostic codes.

6. If you disagree with the VA's rating decision and an Increase Claim is not an option, you can submit a Supplemental Claim, Higher-Level Review, or Board of Veterans' Appeal.

7. Never give up!

TIPS & FAQS

Below are my basic tips for success and frequently asked questions to help you through your VA claims process and *win* your claim.

KMD89'S TIPS FOR SUCCESS

- **Research! Learn! Educate yourself!**
    - ○ Take ownership of your claim and educate yourself on the VA claims process.
    - ○ Research the VA's website, reference the 38 CFR and M21-1, read the instructions on

the needed forms, review the DBQs ahead of any C&P exams, and ask questions.

- **Confirm if you're eligible for benefits based on your character of discharge.**
    - ○ If you have multiple periods of service and the last period is negative, you may still be eligible to receive compensation benefits for your honorable periods of service.
- **Confirm that the disability/diagnosis you're claiming is eligible for compensation under the five ways of service connection:**
    - ○ Pre-service aggravation
    - ○ Direct Service Connection
    - ○ Secondary (condition caused by another service-connected condition)
    - ○ Increase (for a condition already service connected)
    - ○ Presumptive Service Connection (including the PACT Act)
        - ▪ Agent Orange
        - ▪ Gulf War
        - ▪ Camp Lejeune
        - ▪ 1-Year Presumptive
        - ▪ 3-Year Presumptive
        - ▪ 7-Year Presumptive

- **Know the correct evidence to submit with your claim.**

  - Gather the applicable STRs (service treatment records), private medical paperwork, VA progress notes, and Vet Center notes concerning your condition(s).

  - Separate your evidence by condition to make it easy for the VA rater to know what condition each piece of attached evidence pertains to.

  - Ensure you highlight any stressor and/or marker evidence when claiming PTSD for non-combat trauma, personal trauma and/or military sexual trauma (MST).

- **Learn how to properly word the conditions you're claiming.**

  - Know the VA-specific language as it pertains to the conditions and exact rating percentages you're eligible for.

  - If you just tell your story without understanding the terminology, it may be unclear to the VA employees and/or medical examiners exactly what you're claiming and how those conditions are service connected.

- ○ Practice how to talk to the medical examiner ahead of time. Bring notes if you attend a C&P or public DBQ exam.

- **Be prepared to be frustrated, angry, and confused. Many veterans lack a clear understanding of the verbiage in their rating decision, and/or**
  - ○ Why a C&P exam was not requested for a condition(s), or
  - ○ Why a C&P exam was requested when a public DBQ was submitted, or
  - ○ Why a condition was denied for service connection or compensation, and/or
  - ○ Why a particular rating percentage was chosen.

- **Never give up!**
  - ○ The military taught us never to quit. Why should this be any different? Stay in the fight!

KMD89'S FREQUENTLY ASKED QUESTIONS (FAQS)

- **How long do I have to wait to receive my rating decision?**

o   There is no set time when a rating decision will be reached. The VA raters are supposed to work each claim in the order they receive them.

o   Several factors can prolong a claim, such as the amount of evidence the VA rater has to review, or any additional tasks the VA needs to complete during the claim process. Remember to submit only the most relevant evidence and highlight the main information. Make your claim as clear and easy to process as possible.

- **Is there a time limit to file a claim after you leave active duty or separate from the military?**

    o   No, you can file a claim at any time.

    o   Certain conditions under 38CFR 3.309(a) exist for claiming conditions within one year from discharge under the 1-year presumptive claim.

- **Is there a max number of conditions a veteran can claim at once?**

    o   No, but make sure you are clear on what you are claiming and why.

- **Can I file a claim while still on active duty?**

    o   Yes, a service member can file a BDD claim 180 to 90 days from discharge. Check VA's website and M21-1 reference manual for qualifications and criteria (also noted in chapter 2).

- **If I'm still on active duty, should I do an Intent to File?**
  - It's not necessary. The purpose of the Intent to File is to receive backdated benefits. However, if you're still on active duty, your effective date will be the day after your discharge date even if you do an Intent to File before that date.

- **Do I need my medical records from active duty before filing a claim?**
  - No, the VA should have access to them already. Even so, it's good to know what evidence you have of any complaints, diagnoses, treatments, injuries, illnesses, pain, or diseases that are noted in those records. The VA raters are busy and may not see everything.

- **Can I submit a C&P exam (DBQ/disability benefits questionnaire) from my private doctor?**
  - Yes, but be sure to check the VA's website and follow the guidelines on public DBQs. Ensure your medical or mental health professional completes the correct and up-to-date DBQ.

- **What if I have a dishonorable or bad conduct discharge? Can I still file a claim?**
    - o Yes, if you reenlisted or have at least one other period of service that is under honorable conditions.
    - o The last period with a dishonorable or bad conduct discharge may bar you from compensation and treatment with the VA, especially if the condition you're claiming is connected only to that part of your service. However, the other periods would be honorable and therefore eligible for compensation and treatment.
- **Can a family member call the VA's national call center and receive information about my claim?**
    - o Yes, though they must sign and submit a third-party consent form: **VA Form 21-0845** "Authorization to Disclose Personal Information to a Third Party," and it has to be on file before the VBA (Veterans Benefit Administration) will release any information.
- **Is Individual Unemployability (IU) a stand-alone claim?**
    - o No, it's an Increase Claim for the service-connected condition(s) that prevents

you from gainful employment. It's important to do your research and word this type
of claim according to the VA's language.

o   Sometimes it's easier to get to 100% disability than it is to do an IU claim, depending
on your overall compensation percentage
and what conditions you're service connected for.

- **How long does it take to receive my VA claims
folder on CD after I submit my request?**

    o   There is no set time frame. It took the VA
    eleven months to send mine, and I had to
    push the issue by filing a White House VA
    Hotline complaint. But other veterans have
    received a copy of their claims folder in a
    few months.

    o   If you plan to file a Higher-Level Review,
    you only have twelve months (one year) to
    do so from when you received your rating
    decision, so don't wait too long to gather
    needed information to help you prove your
    case.

- **Should I work with a lawyer or Veterans Service
Officer (VSO) to help me with my claim?**

    o   There is no requirement to work with a
    VSO or any other organization, law firm,

company, or individual. The decision is up to you.

o   Hundreds of organizations and legal entities offer services to help veterans with their disability claims. Unfortunately, they are not all created equal. Some may help you, some may not.

o   If you don't take responsibility for your own claim and do the research, you'll never know how much they're really helping you until you get approved or denied and wonder why.

- **What additional compensation or assistance can I receive from the VA?**

   o   If you are service connected, you may qualify for IU (individual unemployability), P&T (permanent and total), or various Special Monthly Compensation (SMC) benefits for you and/or your dependents. Consult 38 CFR 3.340; 3.350(b)(1), (2), & (3); 4.16; and 6.18; and M21-1 VIII. iv.4.A. to learn more, or contact KMD89 VA Claims Consulting®.

APPENDIX:

IMPORTANT RESOURCES

Contact the **<u>Veterans Crisis Line</u>** if you're having suicidal thoughts or need help right away:

- Call: 988 then press 1
- Text: 838255
- Chat online: www.veteranscrisisline.net

Call the **VA benefits hotline/VA national call center** at 1-800-827-1000 to:

- Declare your Intent to File for compensation
- Follow up on your Intent to File
- Ask what C&P exams have been scheduled and for what conditions/DBQs

- Request a disability breakdown letter (summary letter) after you received your rating decision, to include all your service-connected conditions and diagnostic codes, and the rating percentages assigned

Call the **White House VA Hotline** at 1-855-948-2311

- If you feel you have a legitimate complaint and want to file your complaint with a White House VA Hotline representative, who will issue you a reference number (make sure you keep this for your records) and then forward it to the VA for follow-up

STAY CONNECTED WITH KMD89 VA CLAIMS CONSULTING®

Website:

www.kmd89.com

Facebook:

www.facebook.com/
kmd89vaclaimsconsulting

LinkedIn:

www.linkedin.com/in/
dewayne-kimble

Twitter:

twitter.com/kmd89con

Instagram:

www.instagram.com/
kmd89consulting/

YouTube:

www.youtube.com/c/
DewayneKimble?sub_
confirmation=1
Subscribe for updates,
new videos, and monthly
Live Q & A Sessions.

SPEAKER FOR YOUR NEXT EVENT

As a veteran and former VA claims adjudicator, Dewayne Kimble has a deep understanding of the VA claims process and how it impacts the lives of our nation's veterans. He is passionate about helping veterans, service members, and their families navigate this complex system and obtain the VA disability compensation benefits they deserve. With over a decade of expertise in the field, Dewayne has a wealth of knowledge to share with others. He provides invaluable insights and actionable education to help veterans better understand the VA claims process.

Dewayne would be honored to speak to your organization or veteran community. To learn more about the benefits of inviting Dewayne to speak, please visit our site at www.kmd89.com/grouptraining.